MW00439970

RICHARD CAPRIOLA

the

ADDICTED
Child

A PARENT'S GUIDE TO
ADOLESCENT SUBSTANCE ABUSE

The Addicted Child

A Parent's Guide to Adolescent Substance Abuse

Richard Capriola

ISBN (Print Edition): 978-1-09832-723-1

ISBN (eBook Edition): 978-1-09832-724-8

© 2020. All rights reserved. No part of this publication may be reproduced, distributed, or transmitted in any form or by any means, including photocopying, recording, or other electronic or mechanical methods, without the prior written permission of the publisher, except in the case of brief quotations embodied in critical reviews and certain other noncommercial uses permitted by copyright law.

ACKNOWLEDGMENTS

During my tenure with the Menninger Clinic in Houston, Texas, I treated patients on the Adolescent Treatment Unit and the Comprehensive Psychiatric Assessment and Stabilization Unit. Both specialize in assessing and treating patients with psychiatric and substance use disorders.

It was an honor to work alongside a talented staff of psychiatrists, social workers, psychologists, and nurses. They assessed, diagnosed, and treated patients with severe psychiatric and addiction disorders. Because they believed in the untapped strength of each patient, more times than not, this remarkably talented staff transformed lives. It was an honor to be part of their team.

I am also indebted to the patients and families I met. They blessed me with a willingness to share their stories and struggles. I learned far more from them than they learned from me. Their courage to confront serious mental health and substance abuse issues enabled them to move forward with their lives and gave others hope that healing and recovery is possible.

Very few things are more destructive to a family than having someone, especially a child, addicted to drugs or alcohol. While working on the Adolescent Treatment Unit I met parents struggling to understand and accept their child's psychiatric and substance abuse issues. For most of these families it was a heart-breaking experience.

Sadly, many families do not have the financial resources to send their child to a nationally acclaimed psychiatric hospital like the Menninger Clinic. Their desperate search for help often leaves them feeling alone and without a roadmap to guide them through the process of assessment and treatment. *The Addicted Child* was written for these families.

CONTENTS

INTRODUCTION

The Addicted Child

As the parent of an addicted child, feelings of helplessness, blame, and fear can drown out any sense of hope. If your child uses alcohol or drugs, you know firsthand how it affects your family. You may be carrying your child's addiction on your own shoulders. You've cried and felt scared, wondering if today the drug would take your child forever. You might have been angry and asked, "How did I miss the warnings?" or wondered, "What did I do wrong?"

You love your child but, like one patient's mother told me, you may feel overcome with fear. She sat across from me and through her tears, she cried, "I didn't know what to do. I thought I was going to lose her."

If addiction has plagued your family, you see up-close how alcohol and drugs invade your child's brain and create abnormal behaviors. Angry outbursts. Defensiveness. Rebellion. When you try to control these behaviors, you set in motion a conflict that escalates the problem. So you establish strict rules, and when your child violates them, you punish the behavior. Soon you find yourself stuck in a cycle of control and out-of-control. It's easy to become overwhelmed with the battle.

The majority of teens I treated used marijuana, usually multiple times a day. When asked why they used it, most said, "It helps my anxiety." Their answer points to an important clue hidden below the surface of substance abuse: There could be an underlying reason why your child uses alcohol or drugs. It might be to relieve anxiety or depression. Perhaps it's to avoid traumatic memories like bullying. It might be to cope with a psychological issue, such as post-traumatic stress disorder, attention deficit disorder, or a personality disorder. While not every child using substances has an underlying psychological issue, for those that do, treating the alcohol or drug problem without treating the mental health issue behind it can be a treatment plan doomed to fail.

When you look beyond your child's drinking or drug use, you may discover their struggle to manage intolerable thoughts, feelings, or memories is a core issue that requires treatment. However, you're probably not equipped with the resources, training, or education to adequately do so. Therefore, it's important that you insist on a comprehensive psychological and medical assessment before starting any treatment.

If you've been down this road, you might have already taken this step. Hearing the results of your child's psychological assessment and diagnoses can be more difficult than hearing the details of their substance use. No parent wants to hear that their child is "broken." You probably knew something about their alcohol or drug use, but the psychological findings can be shocking. Shattering. Confusing. Frightening.

I have sat in hundreds of diagnostic conferences when parents heard for the first time that their child has severe anxiety, major depression, or suffers from an emerging personality disorder or schizophrenia. Hearing these diagnoses is heartbreaking because parents usually see the substance abuse while completely unaware of the underlying mental health issues.

Your child may be creative at flying under the radar and discreetly hiding their substance use. The most frequent reaction I heard from parents was, "I had no idea this was going on!" Or if they suspected their child was using a substance, they were shocked at how extensive it was. Sometimes it was weekly use. Often it was daily.

There are important differences between adult and adolescent substance use disorders. Unlike the adult brain, your child's brain is a work in process and reaches maturity in their mid-twenties. Thus, introducing alcohol or drugs into their maturing brain puts your child at risk of developing a substance use disorder.

The consequences of substance use are another difference. Adults abusing substances often experience catastrophic consequences, such as losing a job or relationship. Many have been incarcerated. Adolescents, on the other hand, experience few consequences other than the threat of punishment from their parents, which often reinforces their substance use as a form of rebellion.

Discovering your child has a substance abuse problem is not a death sentence. It doesn't have to be the fate of your child. In fact, information truly is power when battling addiction. So we begin our journey with a summary of adolescent substance use. Much of the information in Chapter One and other chapters is borrowed from the University of Michigan's Monitoring the Future study[1] and other sources, as noted. Each year Monitoring the Future surveys students in eighth, tenth, and twelfth grades and reports their use of alcohol and drugs and their opinions on those substances.

Chapter Two explains the neuroscience of substance abuse. Alcohol and drugs have the power to change your child's brain. The chemicals also influence behaviors you probably find unacceptable. This chapter explains how substances work within your child's brain.

Chapter Three describes how psychiatrists, addictions counselors, psychologists, and social workers assess your child. The best treatment starts with a comprehensive assessment, and in this chapter you'll be led through the assessment process.

Chapter Four through Chapter Twelve briefly summarize alcohol and the street drugs used by today's adolescents. You may be unaware of many drugs invading our communities, but these chapters give an overview of them.

Chapter Thirteen explains process disorders like eating behaviors and self-harm. These sometimes accompany alcohol and drug use and can also trap a child who is not using substances. If your child develops a substance use disorder along with a process disorder, it's important that both be assessed and treated.

Chapter Fourteen and Chapter Fifteen describe principles for adolescent substance abuse treatment and treatment options.

Chapter Sixteen identifies evidence-based approaches to treatment. Recovery resources are also provided to help guide you and your child toward healing.

Chapter Seventeen lists resources including references to educational consultants, mental health and substance abuse resources, and information on support groups. Not only does your child need support, but parents do too. It's a difficult road that no parent should have to walk alone. This book's goal is to equip you with what you need to help not only the child you love, but also yourself as you navigate it.

CHAPTER ONE

Adolescent Substance Use

It's a plague that has gripped thousands of lives. For many, a cure felt out of reach. But it's not something new. In fact, illicit drug use among adolescents has remained fairly stable since 2009. About one third of tenth and twelfth graders, and 15 percent of eighth graders, use illicit drugs. These drugs include marijuana, LSD, MDMA (Ecstasy), OxyContin, amphetamines, sedatives, and tranquilizers. Twenty-one years ago, the percentage of adolescents using these drugs was much higher.

Vaping: Vaping stores can be found in almost any town or shopping mall. Because of this, it might seem harmless enough. But since 2017, there's been a dramatic increase in vaping, which involves inhaling a substance from an electronic device like an e-cigarette. These devices have cartridges filled with liquids including nicotine, marijuana, or fruit flavors. The liquid turns into a vapor that's inhaled. *More than 40 percent of seniors and one of every three tenth graders are vaping!* Those are pretty high numbers.

Marijuana: Marijuana is the most widely used illicit drug, especially as it's easily available and accessible. Smoking marijuana is increasing in lower grades and decreasing somewhat among seniors. Marijuana vaping, however, is increasing at alarming rates. Synthetic marijuana use has decreased significantly across all grades since 2011.

Psychotherapeutic Drugs: These are prescription-based drugs used outside of medical supervision. During the 2000s, teens viewed them as less dangerous because they were legally prescribed for legitimate medical reasons, like pain management and for anxiety. Fortunately, their use has declined over the past decade.

Cigarette Smoking: Cigarette use continues to decline and is close to historically low levels. Nicotine vaping, however, is increasing at an alarming rate.

Alcohol: Alcohol is the primary substance used by adolescents. While there has been some decline in drinking, 60 percent of students will have drunk more than just a few sips of alcohol by graduation, and 25 percent will have used alcohol by eighth grade.

SUBGROUP DIFFERENCES[2]

Gender Differences: Boys have higher rates of illicit drug use than girls. While boys previously engaged in higher rates of marijuana use, the difference has virtually been eliminated. Misuse of prescription narcotic drugs is considerably higher among twelfth grade boys. Girls use amphetamines and tranquilizers more than boys in the lower grades.

There's also been a narrowing of gender differences with alcohol. Twelfth grade boys previously reported higher alcohol use rates than girls but the difference is now considerably less. In eighth and tenth grades, there's almost no gender difference. Girls report similar rates of *binge drinking* as males in grades eight and ten, but lower rates than males in twelfth grade.

Race/Ethnicity: There are differences among the three largest racial/ethnic groups in the United States—Whites, African-Americans, and Hispanics. White students have had substantially higher rates of using illicit drugs than African-American students, but this difference has narrowed in recent years because of increasing marijuana use among African-American students and a decline among White students. African-American students engage in lower rates of certain illicit drugs at all three grade levels, in particular hallucinogens, synthetic marijuana, and all forms of prescription drugs used without a doctor's order.

African-American students use alcohol and cigarettes at lower rates than Whites. The Monitoring the Future Study found Hispanic students use of various drugs places them between the other two groups in twelfth grade—usually closer to the rates for Whites than for African-Americans.

College Plans: High school students who claim they are not college-bound (a decreasing proportion of the total youth population over the past years) are at considerably higher risk for using illicit drugs, drinking heavily, and particularly smoking cigarettes.

Socioeconomic Level: The parent's average level of education has been used as a substitute for the socioeconomic status of the family. For many drugs the differences in use among income levels are very small. However, one interesting difference occurs for cocaine, where the use was directly associated with socio-economic level in the early 1980s. In this case, higher parental education levels were associated with higher cocaine use. Since the advent of crack, which offered cocaine at a lower price, that association nearly disappeared by 1986.

Sexual Risk:[3] According to the CDC, "Adolescent substance use is also associated with sexual risk behaviors that put young people at risk for HIV, sexually transmitted diseases (STDs), and pregnancy...Studies conducted among adolescents have identified an association between substance use and sexual risk behaviors such as ever having sex, having multiple sex partners, not using a condom, and pregnancy before the age of fifteen."

Furthermore, researchers found that "as the frequency of substance use increases, the likelihood of sex and the number of sex partners also increases. In addition, studies have shown that sexual risk behaviors increase in adolescents who use alcohol, and are highest among students who use marijuana, cocaine, prescription drugs (such as sedatives, opioids, and stimulants), and other illicit drugs. Adolescents who reported no substance use are the least likely to engage in sexual risk-taking."

Chapter Two

The Brain on Drugs[4]

What does it mean if someone says your child is *addicted*? When you hear the word "addiction," it evokes a lot of confusion and fear. But it's important to keep something in mind: "addiction" is not a diagnosis. It's a term used to stigmatize people in a negative way. Professionals do *not* diagnose a child with "addiction" or being an "addict." The correct diagnosis, if used after testing and assessment, is "Substance Use Disorder," which can range from mild, moderate, to severe.

Not every child using alcohol or drugs develops a substance use disorder. However, even without a substance use disorder, alcohol and drugs can influence your child's behavior and disrupt their life and yours.

Every child is at risk for developing a substance use disorder that almost always begins in childhood. The variables that influence that risk can involve a variety of things including lack of parental supervision, genetic history, social connections, mental health, and exposure to drugs.

Most illicit drug use begins during adolescence, usually between ages fourteen and twenty:

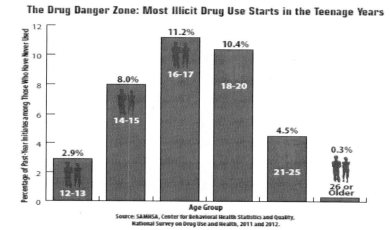

The Drug Danger Zone: Most Illicit Drug Use Starts in the Teenage Years

Brain Development: A child's brain matures from back to front. The prefrontal cortex (highlighted by the circles in the following picture) is one of the last areas to mature. It enables an individual to assess situations and risks, make sound decisions, and keep emotions and desires under control. This area of your child's brain isn't fully developed until around age twenty-five, leaving them more likely to engage in risky behaviors, including alcohol and drug use.

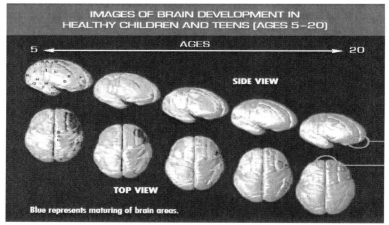

IMAGES OF BRAIN DEVELOPMENT IN
HEALTHY CHILDREN AND TEENS (AGES 5-20)

Blue represents maturing of brain areas.

Source: PNAS 101:8174-8179. 2004.

The brain has about 86 billion neurons (nerve cells) with 100 trillion connections. Neurons "talk" to each other with chemicals called neurotransmitters. A message is sent when a brain cell (neuron) releases a chemical (neurotransmitter) into the space (synapse) between one cell and another. When the connection is made, the neurotransmitter crosses the synapse and attaches to proteins (receptors) on the receiving brain cell.

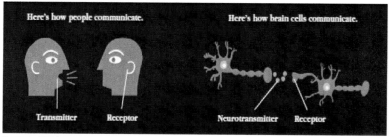

Dopamine is an important neurotransmitter. It regulates emotion and pleasure. It's dopamine that gives your child a pleasurable feeling when using a drug like marijuana. They experience this pleasure, or "high," because dopamine levels increase. The following chart shows how food and sex increase dopamine in the brain to produce pleasurable feelings:

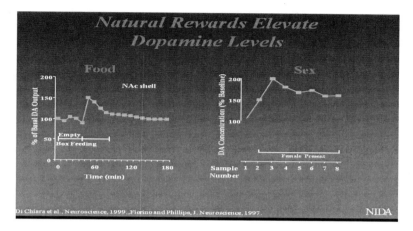

What all illicit drugs have in common is their ability to stimulate the brain to produce large amounts of dopamine, far more than the brain was created to handle. Drugs like amphetamines, cocaine, nicotine, and morphine produce surges of dopamine. This surge of dopamine delivers an intense pleasurable feeling (the high), which reinforces continued drug use.

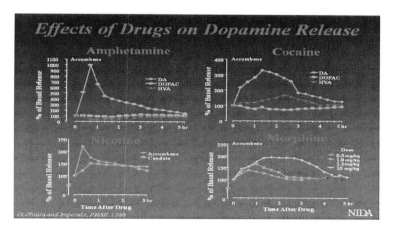

The brain has a "GO" system or reward pathway located deep within the brain and runs between the Ventral Tegmental Area (VTA) and the Nucleus Accumbens. It's called a reward pathway because drugs tend to settle in this area of the brain and the brain views using drugs as a pleasurable and rewarding experience.

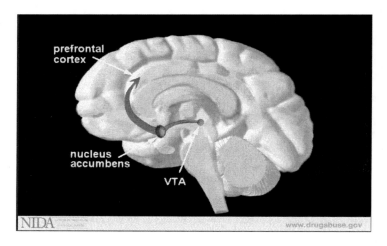

Drugs affect most areas of the brain, but there's a heavy concentration in the reward pathway. The following picture shows marijuana attached to different areas of the brain with heavy concentration in the reward pathway:

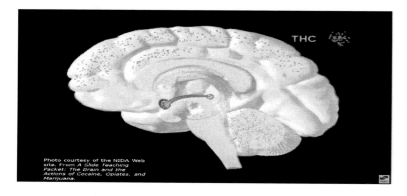

Our brain also has a "STOP" system, the prefrontal cortex. It's responsible for higher order thinking and the ability to weigh advantages and disadvantages in order to make rational decisions. Because this part of your child's brain is not fully developed, their ability to make sound decisions and weigh negative consequences is compromised, especially under the influence of alcohol or drugs.

Without the influence of substances, the "stop" and "go" systems work more effectively. However, under the influence of alcohol or drugs the communication system breaks down. The reward pathway, or "go" system, overrides the prefrontal cortex "stop" system. The go system is screaming "go and seek the drug and get the intense pleasure you experienced the last time you used," while the stop system is whispering "remember what happened the last time you used."

Let's say I like donuts. My brain's pleasure-seeking "go" system is screaming, "Go and eat a dozen donuts" because it remembers that donuts gave me pleasure (a high) and more importantly, eating them *reduced my intense anxiety* (or some other uncomfortable feeling). As I'm considering whether or not to eat those donuts, my brain's rational "stop" system whispers, "Remember the last time you ate a dozen donuts? You gained weight and threw up!"

Drugs short-circuit the brain's stop and go system. It's not that the two systems aren't working. It's more like the "go" system is screaming "Pursue that high," and the "stop" system is whispering, "It's not good for you." Because these two systems have been hijacked by drugs, they aren't communicating effectively and in my analogy, I end up eating a dozen donuts!

This is how your child's brain works under the influence of drugs. *It minimizes the negative consequences of alcohol or drug use in an attempt to seek and achieve a pleasurable experience* (sometimes to escape an unpleasant thought or feeling like anxiety or a painful memory). Does this mean it's too late to fix the stop and go systems within the brain? Not at all! The brain has a remarkable capacity to heal. Once alcohol and drugs stop assaulting the brain, healing and recovery can begin.

CHAPTER THREE

Assessing Your Child

You'll never forget the day you discover your child is drinking alcohol or using drugs. The signs start to show up more often. Their behavior is escalating out of control. They've become defensive, angry, and sometimes combative. The situation is intolerable. You tell yourself, "Enough is enough. Something must be done!" But where do you begin?

In extreme cases when the behavior or drug use becomes life-threatening or dangerous, emergency intervention is required and you should act quickly. Call 911 for help, if necessary. In the event where a life is at risk, your child may be taken to a hospital for treatment and possible admission for stabilization.

In non-emergency situations you should begin with a comprehensive assessment from licensed professionals, including psychiatrists, psychologists, social workers, and addiction counselors. You might also consider admission to an inpatient adolescent program for both assessment and treatment. Your child will likely resist any assessment, but you should insist that it be completed. All successful treatment begins with a comprehensive assessment and diagnoses.

INFORMAL ASSESSMENTS

Teens are always changing. Along with their hormonal changes, you might notice behavioral and personality shifts as they get older. Teens are also naturals at hiding things from their parents. So how do you detect if your child has a substance use disorder? Early signs can go unnoticed, or you might not connect certain behaviors with substance use. You may be the last to learn your child is drinking alcohol or using drugs.

Regardless of your child's attempt to hide their alcohol or drug use, there are warning signs. For example, if your child "starts behaving differently for no apparent reason—such as acting withdrawn, frequently tired or depressed, or hostile—it could be a sign of a developing drug-related problem. Parents and others may overlook such signs, believing them to be a normal part of puberty."[5] Other warning signs include:[6]

- a change in peer group;
- carelessness with grooming;
- decline in academic performance;
- missing classes or skipping school;
- loss of interest in favorite activities;
- changes in eating or sleeping habits;
- deteriorating relationships with family members or friends.

If you suspect your child is using alcohol or drugs, you should obtain a comprehensive assessment from a team of licensed professionals. This team includes psychiatrists, social workers, psychologists, and addictions counselors. It's important that you choose a team experienced with adolescent substance use and mental health. If you don't know where to start the assessment process, ask your primary care physician for referrals.

COMPREHENSIVE ASSESSMENTS

A comprehensive assessment goes deeper than an informal assessment. These assessments involve a full medical examination, psychological testing, detailed substance use history, and if needed, consults for eating disorders, self-harm, and other process disorders like computer gaming. When the assessments are completed by a team of professionals, diagnoses and a treatment plan can be recommended.

A medical assessment involves a complete physical examination including blood work, urine analysis, drug screens, EEG, EKG, and other exams to determine the overall health of your child, and any negative impact substance use may have already made. One new assessment is the Genecept Assay. It's a simple cheek swab that examines eighteen genes within the DNA to predict your child's response to medications. It narrows the range of effective medications and reduces the trial-and-error approach to medication management. Twenty-five percent of patients tested with the Genecept Assay have been children and adolescents. Information is available on the Genomind website at https://genomind.com.

Psychological assessments by licensed psychologists and neuropsychologists involve cognitive and personality testing.

You should insist on a comprehensive psychological assessment to identify any psychological issues that might be problematic.

A substance abuse assessment includes testing and a detailed history of your child's substance use. This captures the history, frequency, and extent of substances used. Clinicians will likely use the Substance Abuse Subtle Screening Inventory (SASSI). The adult version was published in 1985 and the adolescent version in 1990. The adolescent SASSI, for ages twelve through eighteen, predicts whether your child has a high probability of a substance use disorder and whether it's mild, moderate, or severe.

A psychosocial assessment is usually completed by a licensed social worker. It includes a review of your child's developmental history, family systems overview, family psychological history, and a social system review, which collects information about their friends and social environment. The information is usually obtained by interviewing parents.

The stage of change assessment[7] identifies how prepared your child is to change their substance abuse behaviors. "Perhaps the most well-known and empirically validated modes of 'readiness to change' is *the transtheoretical model* (DiClemente and Prochaska, 1998). It identifies five stages of change. People usually move back and forth between stages and cycle through them at different rates." The five primary stages of change explain how an individual moves through the decision process of changing a behavior: precontemplation, contemplation, preparation, action, and maintenance. Most of my adolescent patients were in the precontemplation or contemplation stage.

The precontemplation stage involves denial. Teens in this stage may not have experienced adverse consequences and rarely see their substance use as a problem. The majority of adolescents I treated were stuck in this stage. They either minimized their substance use or claimed it was helpful and denied any negative consequences.

Tony is an example of a teen firmly planted in precontemplation. His diagnosis included cannabis substance use disorder. Tony smoked before school and left campus during lunch to smoke, then smoked again after school. He denied any negative consequences from smoking. During our first session Tony made his position very clear, "I like smoking dope. What's the big deal? I'm not stopping and it's not hurting anybody."

In the contemplation stage teens are ambivalent, simultaneously seeing reasons to change and reasons not to change. They continue using substances, but will consider stopping or reducing their use. *For an adolescent abusing alcohol or drugs, moving from the precontemplation to the contemplation stage is a huge move!* Once your child advances to the contemplation stage, the foundation is set for constructive treatment.

The preparation stage involves a decision to change. In this stage your child compares the advantages and disadvantages of ending their substance use. When they believe the advantages are more important than the disadvantages, their attitude is likely to change. However, it's crucial that they move forward from the preparation stage into the next step: taking action.

The action stage involves making efforts to change a behavior. In this stage your child might be in an adolescent treatment program or working with a counselor and attending an adolescent therapy or support group. This is where you start to see improvement and growth.

The maintenance stage involves taking action to maintain the changes made. Once your child is sober, it's imperative they continue treatment to maintain it.

A relapse is a return to substance use. Your child may intentionally relapse or be caught in situations or intense emotions that overwhelm them, which can lead to using alcohol or drugs for immediate relief. If your child relapses, it's important to note if they were honest and forthcoming about it. There's a big difference between a child who hides or lies about a relapse and one who honestly admits to the relapse, either voluntarily or when confronted.

If your child admits a relapse, it opens the door for a learning experience. Together you can explore the causes of the relapse and options for better decisions in the future. *If you can help your child turn a relapse into a learning experience rather than a failure, you lessen the chance it will happen again.*

Diagnosing your child can be a lengthy, intense process.[8] A diagnosis describes a condition like anxiety, depression, post-traumatic stress disorder, or a personality disorder. The criteria are listed in the *Diagnostic and Statistical Manual of Mental Disorders (DSM)*. The *DSM* was updated in 2013 to delete terms like substance abuse and substance dependence. A new diagnosis of Substance Use Disorder (SUD) was created. It has three qualifiers: mild, moderate, and severe. For example, your child might receive a diagnosis of alcohol SUD (moderate) or cannabis

SUD (severe). Whether your child fits into the mild, moderate, or severe category is based on the number of symptoms present. As the number of symptoms increases, the diagnosis rises from mild to moderate to severe. The symptoms include:

- taking a substance in larger amounts or over a longer period of time than intended;

- persistent desire/unsuccessful attempts to cut down or control use;

- spending a great deal of time to obtain, use, or recover from a substance;

- strong desires or cravings to use a substance;

- recurrent use resulting in the failure to fulfill major obligations at work, school, or home;

- continued use despite recurrent social or interpersonal problems (such as arguments) caused by the use;

- ending or curtailing social-recreational activities because of substance use;

- using a substance in hazardous situations;

- continued use despite knowing it's causing physical/ psychological problems;

- exhibiting symptoms of tolerance that can include: requiring more of a substance over time to get the desired effect, or using the same amount of a substance no longer gives the desire effect;

- exhibiting withdrawal symptoms or using a substance to relieve/avoid withdrawal.

Diagnoses are necessary labels we give patients. Learning your child's diagnoses can be both a relief and heartbreaker. I've sat in hundreds of diagnostic conferences where family members first learned of their child's mental health and substance use diagnoses. It's never easy to hear someone say your child has a serious psychological and/or substance use disorder.

On one hand, you feel relieved with answers to your child's behavior. On the other hand, you feel the pain of their suffering and their struggle to cope with what are often intolerable feelings or thoughts. You wish you could save them, but you feel helpless. These are common reactions when professionals describe your child in clinical terms. However, if your child is "labeled" with a substance use or psychiatric disorder, *it does not define them*. *The purpose of a diagnosis is to identify a course of treatment and set the groundwork for recovery and maintenance.*

CHAPTER FOUR

Marijuana[9]

Weed. Pot. Reefer. Marijuana goes by many names, and it's also the most commonly used drug among adolescents. Much like how cigarette smokers rely on hits of nicotine throughout the day, a majority of teens I treated smoked marijuana multiple times a day. They saw little or no risk in using the drug and believed it relieved their anxiety. Most did not want to reduce or end their use.

You might be surprised to learn your child is smoking marijuana. Discovering they are using can be scary, but they are not likely to die from an overdose. They are much more likely to get injured by doing something under its influence, like driving a car, swimming, or skateboarding. However, most teens prefer to relax, hang out with their friends, and smoke.

The percentage of tenth and twelfth graders using marijuana is higher than it was ten years ago. Over one in four tenth graders and over one third of seniors smoke marijuana. Furthermore, **vaping** marijuana has increased at an alarming rate.

Is marijuana difficult to find? You may be surprised at its accessibility. Seventy-eight percent of seniors say it's either fairly easy or very easy to obtain. Thirty-three percent of eighth graders say the same thing.

Only a small percentage of seniors believe smoking marijuana involves great risk. Fifteen percent say smoking marijuana *occasionally* poses a great risk and only 30 percent believe *regular* marijuana use is a great risk.

While some believe smoking marijuana is harmless, research suggests that "about 30 percent of people who use marijuana have some level of marijuana use disorder even if they are not yet addicted." Also, a person is more likely to develop a marijuana use disorder if they begin using the drug as an adolescent rather than as an adult.

The risk of abusing or becoming dependent on marijuana is age dependent. Meaning, the younger a person is, the more likely they will abuse or become dependent on it:

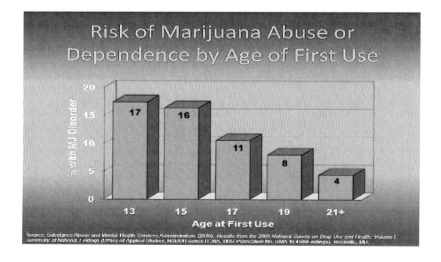

There are many factors that influence the likelihood of a person picking up their first marijuana joint and adolescents use it for different reasons. Some use it to fit in with friends. Others seek the drug out of curiosity or submit to peer pressure. Many, like the majority of my patients, use it to relieve anxiety or some other intolerable feeling.

To best understand what you're dealing with, it's important to know what marijuana is. It consists of the dried leaves, flowers, stems, and seeds from the *Cannabis sativa* or *Cannabis Indica* plant, and it's often rolled into a cigarette and smoked. Sativa has a stimulating effect and Indica is sedating. Cannabis and marijuana have the same meaning and contain a mind-altering chemical called *delta-9-tetrahydrocannabinol,* or THC. Some legal oils on the market known as Cannabidiol or CBD have minimal THC levels and will not get a person high.

Marijuana wrapped with cigarette paper is called a "joint." A "spliff" is like a joint but contains both tobacco and marijuana. A "blunt" is marijuana made with a cigarillo or cigar wrap and because of its size holds more marijuana than a joint or spliff.

Marijuana can be smoked in a pipe or water pipe called a "bong." About 20 percent of tenth and twelfth graders and 7 percent of eighth graders "vape" marijuana using an electronic vaporizer like an e-cigarette. Not only can it be smoked and vaped, but it can be eaten as well. Edibles include marijuana baked goods, some common choices being brownies and cookies, and an assortment of gummies.

Sarah was fifteen years old when admitted for depression, anxiety, and marijuana use. During our first session she shared an event just prior to her admission. She baked a batch of cookies laced with marijuana while her parents were shopping and set them on a table to cool. Her dog found the cookies and helped himself. When Sarah's parents returned home, they found their dog sleeping in a corner. They asked Sarah why the dog was sleeping in the middle of the day, barely able to wake up. She said she had taken him for a long run and he was tired, and her parents bought the story. While it might have seemed like a simple lie, it was a red flag to Sarah's deeper unresolved issues.

I saw patients, both adolescents and adults, who smoked marijuana multiple times a day. Some experienced psychotic events including paranoia, hallucinations, and thought disorders. High doses of marijuana pose greater risks, including panic attacks "or even acute psychosis—thinking that is detached from reality—sometimes including hallucinations. In people who already have the severe mental illness schizophrenia (involving symptoms such as hallucinations, paranoia, and disorganized thinking), marijuana use can worsen its symptoms." More importantly, early marijuana use may increase the risk of psychotic disorders among those who are genetically predisposed to these disorders.

Anyone using marijuana with a history of schizophrenia, paranoia, or hallucinations may be playing Russian roulette with their brain. I don't know when the gun will go off, but I'm pretty sure it may only be a matter of time before it does and they relapse into another psychotic event.

Most adolescents are unaware of marijuana's impact on their brain. In a "Truth Poll" by the National Institute on Drug

Abuse, 30 percent said they really didn't know how marijuana affects their brain and 21 percent said "maybe" they really didn't know:

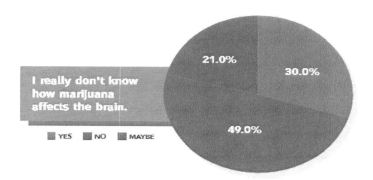

One third (34 percent) said they had or maybe had friends who have tried to talk them into smoking marijuana:

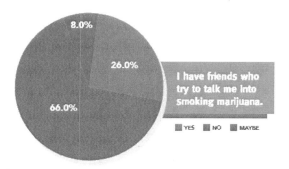

It's telling when you see the stats on why teens keep substance use a secret from their parents. Fear of being judged by their parents discourages 57 percent of adolescents from talking about their substance use:

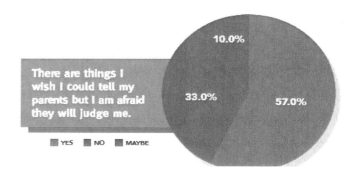

My patients routinely completed a psychological assessment, including cognitive and personality testing. Many with chronic marijuana use showed above average to superior IQ scores. However, their short-term memory was impaired and their brain's processing speed was compromised. Was this due only to marijuana? Probably not. However, marijuana may have contributed to the decline. Also, most patients said marijuana significantly curtailed their motivation.

Challenging these very intelligent teens to stop using a drug they believed helped their anxiety was an exercise in futility. Lecturing them was a waste of time, and telling them the drug was illegal meant nothing. They'd heard it all before. What did they respond to? Neuroscience education! After I explained how drugs like marijuana worked inside their developing brain, I had their attention—and it was a catalyst to change.

When my patients insisted they wouldn't stop using marijuana, I found it pointless to argue with them. Instead, I acknowledged their belief that the drug helped them cope. If their testing showed a decline in their brain's processing speed, I showed them the data. If they acknowledged that smoking marijuana curtailed their motivation (most agreed that it had) I challenged them to consider doing an experiment. They would agree to stay off marijuana for three to six months and then get retested. I was betting that their brain's processing speed and their motivation would significantly improve.

Most teens accepted the challenge because I wasn't demanding they permanently give up the drug, at least not right away. My challenge put control and accountability in their hands. The agreement to suspend smoking marijuana was probably the best I could hope for. If they were able to suspend their use, I was betting they'd feel better, their motivation and attention would improve, and their chance of relapsing would be significantly less.

Synthetic marijuana, called K2 or spice, is a variation that consists of several human-made mind-altering chemicals. These chemicals act on the same brain cells as regular marijuana but are more powerful and unpredictable. Synthetic marijuana ingredients are not consistent among products and emergency rooms report increasing numbers of young people appearing with such symptoms as rapid heart rate, vomiting, and negative mental responses, including hallucinations. With no way to monitor what goes in the product, there's no way to predict the range of symptoms one might experience.

How do you know if your child is using marijuana? The National Institute on Drug Abuse recommends that parents keep aware of changes in their child's behavior. This can be something as minor as in my previous example of Sarah saying she walked the dog to the point of exhaustion. Does walking the dog fit Sarah's routine? Does the dog seem exhausted, or something else? Other changes could include not brushing hair or teeth, skipping showers, changes in mood, challenging relationships with family members, and a change in friends. In addition, declining grades, skipping classes or missing school, loss of interest in sports or other favorite activities, changes in eating or sleeping habits, and getting in trouble in school or with law enforcement could all be related to drug use, or it may indicate other problems. If your child is using marijuana, The National Institute on Drug Abuse believes they might:

- seem unusually giggly and/or uncoordinated;
- have very red, bloodshot eyes or use eye drops often;
- have a hard time remembering things that just
- happened;
- have drugs or drug paraphernalia—possibly
- claiming they belong to a friend;
- have strangely smelling clothes or bedroom;
- use incense and other deodorizers;
- wear clothing or jewelry or have posters that
- promote drug use;
- have unexplained lack of money or extra cash on hand."

Children often look to parents for help and guidance in working through problems, in navigating relationships, and in making decisions, including the decision not to use drugs. But what do you say if you've used drugs in the past? This is where you can use your experience to show how it negatively impacted your life—and you can relate to what they are going through. Even if you have used drugs in the past, you can have an open conversation about the dangers. Whether or not you tell your child about your past drug use is a personal decision, but experience can better equip you to teach others by drawing on the value of past mistakes. You can explain that marijuana is significantly more potent now and that we know a lot more about the potential harmful effects of marijuana on the developing brain, and it's not a risk worth taking.

The National Institute on Drug Abuse offers the following "Tips for Parents":

- Be a good listener.
- Set clear expectations about drug and alcohol use, including real consequences.
- Help your child deal with peer pressure to use drugs.
- Get to know your child's friends and their parents.
- Monitor you child's whereabouts.
- Supervise teen activities.
- Talk to you children often.
- Ensure these discussions focus on how much you care about your child's health.

With the right personal approach and knowledge about the risks, you can help prevent your child from starting on a devastating path toward substance use.

CHAPTER FIVE

Alcohol

Alcohol may be the first substance your child uses. It's easily accessible, perhaps even in your own home, and can appear less risky. The reality of the dangers of alcohol use, however, is quite the contrary. If you discover your child is drinking, you may be alarmed and frightened, and for good reason. The Centers for Disease Control and Prevention estimates that excessive drinking accounts for more than 4,300 deaths each year among underage youth.[10] The National Institute on Alcohol Abuse and Alcoholism rates underage drinking a serious public health problem.

By age fifteen nearly 33 percent of teens have had at least one drink, and by eighteen about 60 percent have had at least one drink. Even more alarming is that 11 percent of all alcohol consumed in the United States is by people ages twelve through twenty, and 90 percent of their drinking is binge drinking.[11]

Jack was admitted to the hospital with a history of anxiety, self-injury, marijuana, and alcohol abuse. He's an example of teens hiding their drinking, sometimes right under the nose of their parents. Jack's parents kept their liquor in an unlocked cabinet. When he wanted alcohol, Jack stole gin or vodka because both are clear liquids. He'd take part of the alcohol from a bottle and replace it with water, so his parents never discovered Jack raiding the liquor cabinet. Not until it was almost too late.

Over one half of twelfth graders report drinking alcohol. Among eighth and tenth graders the numbers are much less at 19 and 38 percent. Nearly one third of twelfth graders and one in five tenth graders have been drunk. While these percentages seem high, they're lower than in 2010, when the numbers were much higher.

Teens don't associate risk with drinking. Only one in five seniors believe having one or two drinks nearly every day is a great risk. Less than half say having five drinks or more once or twice each weekend is a great risk.

If your child wants alcohol, chances are they'll find it. Over 66 percent of sophomores and 83 percent of seniors say it's "fairly easy" or "very easy" to get alcohol. Nearly 50 percent of eighth graders said the same thing.

Parental monitoring and their attitude about drinking "have been shown to be very important influences on under-age drinking. Studies show that some parenting practices have proven beneficial in reducing adolescent alcohol use...Parental monitoring, communication, and emotional support have a positive effect on adolescent alcohol use and are predictive of reduced adolescent alcohol use."[12] In fact, one study found that "parental disapproval of any alcohol use during high school is correlated with reduced alcohol use in college."[13]

While some parents believe providing alcohol in the home with supervision leads to moderate drinking, numerous studies found that parental endorsement of alcohol use was associated with increased adolescent alcohol use, along with heavy episodic drinking and higher rates of alcohol problems into adulthood.[14]

If you discover your child is drinking, it can leave you feeling anxious and helpless. You may end up frustrated trying to control their drinking. However, there's an important role you can play in shaping your child's attitude toward drinking[15]. The National Institute on Alcohol Abuse and Alcoholism suggests that parents: (1) talk about the dangers of drinking, (2) serve as positive role models, (3) not make alcohol available, (4) get to know your children's friends, (5) connect with other parents about sending clear messages about the importance of not drinking alcohol, (6) drink responsibly, if you choose to drink, and (7) supervise all parties to make sure there is no alcohol provided.

If you suspect your child is drinking, what signs should you look for? The Substance Abuse and Mental Health Services Administration recommends the following:[16]

- mood changes, including flare-ups of temper, irritability, and defensiveness;

- school problems, such as poor attendance, low grades, and repeated disciplinary action;

- rebellion against family rules;

- friend changes, such as switching friends, and a reluctance to let you meet new friends;

- a "nothing matters" attitude, sloppy appearance,

- and lack of involvement in past activities;
- general low energy;
- alcohol presence, like finding it in your child's room or backpack or smelling it on breath; and
- memory lapses, poor concentration, bloodshot
- eyes, and slurred speech.

If you notice several warning signs at the same time, or they occur suddenly or are extreme, your child may have a drinking problem. You may wonder what went wrong. You might ask what you could have done to prevent it. However, there are treatment programs and valuable mental health and substance abuse support programs to help you and your child. Suggestions on these programs and groups can be found in the chapter on resources at the end of this book.

CHAPTER SIX

Nicotine

Nicotine comes in many different forms, including cigarettes, smokeless tobacco, and vaping. Cigarette smoking usually begins in adolescence. Less than 6 percent of seniors smoke cigarettes, and less than 4 percent of eighth and tenth graders do so. These figures are significantly lower than in 1996, when over a third of seniors were smoking cigarettes and more than one in five eighth and tenth graders were doing so. About 8 percent of seniors smoke small cigars compared to 23 percent in 2010.

Snuff and chew are smokeless tobacco. Snuff "is finely ground tobacco usually sold in tins, either loose or in packets. It's held in the mouth between the lip or cheek and the gums. Chew is a leafy form of tobacco, usually sold in pouches. It, too, is held in the mouth and may, as the name implies, be chewed."[17]

The nicotine in snuff and chew "is absorbed by the mucous membranes of the mouth... Snus (rhymes with goose) is a relatively new variation of smokeless tobacco, as are some other dissolvable tobacco products that literally dissolve in the mouth."[18] Smokeless tobacco use, like cigarette use, has declined since 1996. Less than 4 percent of students use smokeless tobacco.

While cigarette smoking has declined, *nicotine vaping is increasing at an alarming rate.* One of every three seniors vape nicotine. Sixteen percent of eighth graders and 30 percent of tenth graders are now vaping as it's growing in popularity and accessibility.

Electronic cigarettes (e-cigarettes) are "battery operated devices that people use to inhale an aerosol, which typically contains nicotine (though not always), flavorings, and other chemicals. They can resemble traditional tobacco cigarettes, cigars, or pipes, or even everyday items like pens or USB memory sticks."[19] These devices "are now the most commonly used form of tobacco among youth in the United States."[20]

One popular e-cigarette is the JUUL, which looks like a USB drive. About 15 percent of eighth graders and 28 percent of tenth and twelfth graders use a JUUL.

When it comes to helping your teen avoid or quit using tobacco, there are several steps you can take:[21]

Set an example. Choose not to smoke or use other tobacco products. In addition to modeling desirable behavior, this would prevent your child's exposure to secondhand smoke, which can cause many of the same negative health effects that adolescents would experience if they smoked themselves, including lung disease and asthma.

Don't be shy. Speak up about your concerns before your child begins smoking or if tobacco use of any kind is suspected. Those who do not use tobacco before the age of twenty-six are likely to never start.

Go the distance to prevent secondhand smoke exposure. In addition to not smoking yourself, you can prevent adolescents' exposure to secondhand smoke by not allowing anyone to smoke anywhere in or near your home. Don't allow smoking in the cars they ride in, even with a window down.

Monitor your child. The amount of monitoring you do, such as having expectations about when your teen will be home and checking on their plans, can lessen your teen's risk of nicotine dependence.

Strongly disapprove nicotine. Adolescents whose parents or other adults in their lives strongly disapprove of smoking—even if the adults themselves smoke—are less likely to take up smoking. Parental disapproval has even been found to counteract the influence of peers on smoking.

Enlist allies. Other adults in your child's life, such as teachers, grandparents, aunts, and uncles, influence whether teens start using tobacco, and whether they stop. These adults can be important allies in communicating a no-smoking message to your child.

One valuable resource you might find helpful is Smokefree Teen. It's part of the National Cancer Institute's smokefree.gov initiative. The website has a quit vaping link and smoke-free text program for teens. There is also a link to a quick-start app that offers teens free tips along with inspiration and challenges. The website is **https://teen.smokefree.gov.**

CHAPTER SEVEN

Narcotics[22]

Often considered the deadliest and most addictive of substances, narcotics are opioids. They dull senses and relieve pain. Examples include heroin and pharmaceutical drugs like OxyContin, Vicodin, codeine, morphine, and fentanyl. Teens buy them from drug dealers and friends, or steal them from their own medicine cabinets. They're available in tablets, capsules, patches, powder, and liquids and can be swallowed, smoked, sniffed, or injected. The Centers for Disease Control and Prevention believes 130 people die every day from an opioid overdose.

Opioids produce a general sense of contentedness by reducing tension, anxiety, and aggression, but they come with a variety of unwanted effects, including drowsiness, inability to concentrate, and apathy. Chronic use causes dependence, and when trying to quit, a user will likely experience extreme withdrawal symptoms.

Fentanyl is a powerful opioid and was first developed in 1959, then introduced in the market during 1960s as an intravenous anesthetic. While it is legally manufactured and distributed in the United States, it is 100 times more potent than morphine and 50 times more potent than heroin as an analgesic, or pain reliever. It's responsible for a large number of opioid overdoses. Fentanyl is available in lozenges called "lollipops," sublingual tablets, nasal sprays, transdermal patches, and injections.

Most users abuse it via injection, snorting, sniffing, smoking, or taking it in pill or tablet form. Patches are abused by removing the gel contents and then injecting or ingesting them. Patches can also be frozen, cut into pieces, and placed under the tongue or in the cheek cavity, where it is absorbed into the bloodstream. In addition to producing euphoria it can carry a number of nasty side-effects including confusion, nausea and vomiting

Heroin[23] is a highly addictive rapid-acting opioid. It's processed from morphine and can appear as a white or brown powder, or a black sticky substance called black tar heroin. Other common street names for heroin include big H, horse, hell dust, and smack. It can be injected, sniffed, snorted, or smoked. Mixing heroin with crack cocaine is called *speedballing.*

What makes heroin so dangerous is that it "enters the brain rapidly and binds to opioid receptors on cells located in many areas, especially those involved in feelings of pain and pleasure and in controlling heart rate, sleeping and breathing."[24]

Short-term effects include dry mouth, a warm flush of the skin, heavy feeling in the arms and legs, nausea and vomiting, severe itching, and clouded mental functioning.[25]

The long-term effects are much more severe, including insomnia, collapsed veins for people who inject the drug, damaged tissue inside the nose for people who sniff or snort it, infection of the heart lining and valves, constipation, and lung complications including pneumonia.[26]

Michelle was seventeen when admitted to the hospital for the first time. Her boyfriend introduced her to OxyContin and then heroin. But her drug use didn't just put her at risk, because she was pregnant. There was little we could do for Michelle other than manage her withdrawal symptoms and stabilize her for residential treatment. Within two weeks we placed her in an excellent treatment facility in California. Michelle is an example of a complicated substance use disorder so severe that long-term residential treatment was her best option to save her life and that of her baby.

The percentage of teens using heroin is small and has declined since 2010, when almost 1 percent of students were using it. Today less than .5 percent use heroin, although 17 percent of seniors say the drug is fairly easy or very easy to get.

Luckily, over time "students have long seen heroin to be one of the most dangerous drugs, which helps to account for both the consistently high level of personal disapproval of use and the low prevalence of use."[27] Over 90 percent of twelfth graders disapprove using heroin.

Prescription opioids[28] relax the body and relieve pain and can produce a "high" feeling. Common prescription opioids are hydrocodone (Vicodin), oxycodone (OxyContin, Percocet), oxymorphone (Opana), morphine, codeine, and fentanyl. Teens commonly crush pills or open capsules then snort the powder. They also dilute the powder with water to inject. "Nearly 80 percent of Americans using heroin (including those in treatment) reported misusing prescription opioids prior to using heroin."[29] This direct link between opioids and heroin shows just how risky the backslide can be when entertaining any kind of drug use.

The way opioids work is they "bind to and activate opioid receptors on cells located in many areas of the brain, spinal cord, and other organs in the body, especially those involved in feelings of pain and pleasure. When opioids attach to these receptors, they block pain signals sent from the brain to the body and release large amounts of dopamine throughout the body. This release can strongly reinforce the act of taking the drug, making the user want to repeat the experience."[30]

About 1 percent of eighth graders and 2 percent of tenth and twelfth graders use oxycontin. This is down from 2005 when 1.8 percent of eighth graders, 3.2 percent of tenth graders and 5.5 percent of twelfth graders reported using it. About 1 percent of students use Vicodin.

If you have prescription medications in your home, please secure them from your child. Adolescents can easily raid the family medicine cabinet. Sometimes they steal only a small amount, knowing you're unlikely to notice. In order to keep your child safe, keep your medicines inaccessible.

Chapter Eight

Stimulants

Stimulants, also called "uppers," increase mental and physical processes. Prescriptions like Adderall, Concerta, and Ritalin treat attention and hyperactivity disorders. Cocaine and methamphetamine are non-prescription stimulants.

Cocaine[31] is one such stimulant that has a high potential for abuse. As a street drug, cocaine appears as a fine, white crystalline powder and is known by many names, including coke, C, snow, powder, or blow. Street dealers often dilute (or cut) it with non-psychoactive substances such as cornstarch, talcum powder, flour, or baking soda to increase their profits. When combined with heroin it's called a *speedball.*

Users abuse two forms of cocaine: the water-soluble hydrochloride salt and the water-insoluble cocaine base (or freebase). They inject or snort the hydrochloride salt, which is a powder, but the base form of cocaine is created by processing the drug with ammonia or baking soda and water, then heating it—often using a spoon and a lighter—to remove the hydrochloride to produce a smokable substance.[32] The term *crack* is the street name given to freebase cocaine, and refers to the crackling sound heard when the mixture is heated and then smoked. Crack is more powerful than powder cocaine.

The cocaine high begins quickly and can last up to fifteen minutes. The user then experiences an intense craving for more. Short-term effects include dilated pupils, intense euphoria, decreased appetite, anxiety, paranoia, and aggressive behavior.

Cocaine is highly addictive. It's use among teens has declined significantly since 2000 when 5 percent of seniors were using the drug. Today the numbers have dropped to 2 percent using it. Crack cocaine use has remained stable at 1 percent for seniors since 2009.

During the 1970s the perceived risk of using cocaine fell as the drug's use increased. Use stabilized during the first half of the 1980s, jumped sharply from 1986 and 1987, and then began a substantial decline when the realities of the dangers had set in.

"The year 1986 was marked by a media frenzy over crack cocaine and the widely publicized role of cocaine in the death of Len Bias, a National Basketball Association first-round draft pick. Bias' death was originally reported as resulting from his first experience with cocaine. Though that was later proven to be incorrect, the message had already 'taken'... this event helped to persuade many young people that use of cocaine at any level is dangerous, no matter how healthy the individual."[33]

Methamphetamine[34] is a powerful, highly addictive stimulant that affects the central nervous system. It goes by the names meth, blue, ice, and crystal, among others, and it takes the form of a white, odorless, bitter-tasting crystalline powder that easily dissolves in water or alcohol. It differs from amphetamine in that, at comparable doses, much greater amounts of the drug impact the brain, making it a more potent stimulant. The high lasts longer, but evidence shows it's more harmful to the central nervous system. It can be smoked, snorted, injected, or taken orally.

Smoking or injecting methamphetamine quickly puts the drug into the bloodstream and brain, causing an immediate, intense rush that amplifies the drug's addiction potential and adverse health consequences. The rush, or flash, lasts only a few minutes and is described as extremely pleasurable. Snorting, while not as immediate a high, produces effects within three to five minutes, and oral ingestion produces effects within fifteen to twenty minutes.

Meth is often misused in a 'binge and crash' pattern, where the pleasurable effects disappear before the drug concentration in the blood falls significantly. This causes users to try to maintain the high by taking more of the drug to stave off the crash.

As a powerful stimulant even in small doses, meth increases wakefulness and physical activity and decreases appetite. Users have been diagnosed with a variety of cardiovascular problems, including rapid heart rate, irregular heartbeat, and increased blood pressure. Overdoses can result in elevated body temperature and convulsions that if left untreated can result in death.

If your child is using meth, you might notice significant anxiety, confusion, insomnia, mood disturbances, and violent behavior. These can be accompanied by a number of psychotic features, including paranoia, visual and auditory hallucinations, and delusions. Psychotic symptoms can sometimes last for months or years after a person has quit using the drug.

Less than 1 percent of teens use meth, but even that is too many lives chained to this deadly drug. That's significantly less than in 1999 when nearly 5 percent of tenth and twelfth graders used it.

Bath salts (synthetic cathinones)[35] are man-made stimulants. Less than 1 percent of students use them.

Bath salts are white or brown crystal-like powders sold in plastic or foil packages labeled "not for human consumption." They can be labeled as bath salts, plant food, jewelry cleaner, or phone screen cleaner. They're sold as cheaper substitutes for other stimulants. They can be swallowed, smoked, or injected. Brand names include Bliss, Cloud Nine, Lunar Wave, Vanilla Sky, and White Lightning. New brands tend to be introduced into the market in quick succession to dodge or hinder law enforcement efforts to address their manufacture and sale.

The side effects can induce paranoia, hallucinations, increased friendliness and sex drive, panic attacks and extreme delirium, extreme agitation, and violent behavior.

While the word *salts* might confuse some people, bath salts are not like Epsom salts used in baths. Bathing products have no mind-altering ingredients.

Kratom[36]comes from a tropical tree native to Southeast Asia. Using its leaves produces stimulant effects in low doses that include increased alertness, physical energy, and talkativeness, and sedative effects in high doses, but prolonged use can lead to psychotic symptoms and psychological and physiological dependence. Kratom is mostly abused by oral ingestion in the form of a tablet, capsule, or oil extract.

Prescription stimulants[37] are medicines used to treat attention-deficit hyperactivity disorder (ADHD) and narcolepsy, which produces uncontrollable episodes of deep sleep. These drugs can increase alertness, attention, and energy. Brand name examples are Adderall, Ritalin, Dexedrine, and Concerta. They're also used to improve mental performance. For example, students sometimes misuse them to help cope with late-night studying to get better exam grades, and older adults misuse them to try to improve memory.

Prescription stimulants are some of the most abused stimulants by teens. In addition to abusing them, they will sell them to other students. Others use them to study for final exams or complete a major assignment.

Stimulants are abused by crushing tablets or opening capsules and swallowing the medication or dissolving the powder in water and injecting it. Some teens snort or smoke the powder. Users report a feeling of euphoria, and at high enough doses, prescription stimulants can lead to a dangerously high body temperature, irregular heartbeat, heart failure, and seizures.

Since 2001, nonmedical Ritalin use has declined significantly. *Also, students abuse Adderall more than Ritalin.* Four percent of seniors abuse Adderall whereas 1 percent abuse Ritalin. The difference may be due to Adderall being more widely prescribed because it stays in the body longer than Ritalin. While medically prescribed drugs have their benefits when properly used, they should never be taken outside of their intended use.

CHAPTER NINE

Depressants[38]

You might think that the goal of taking drugs is to feel better, to achieve a high. If that's the case, why would anyone want to take a depressant? It all depends on what the user wants to feel.

The use of depressants grew in popularity as they became more widely accessible. Prescription depressants include sedatives, tranquilizers, and hypnotics. They slow brain activity and are useful for treating anxiety, panic, acute stress reactions, and sleep disorders, common issues among substance users. Benzodiazepines such as Valium, Klonopin, and Xanax are included in this group. Non-benzodiazepine sedatives include Ambien, Lunesta, and Sonata.

Sedative use rose slightly from 2000 to 2005 when 7 percent of seniors claimed to take them. Since then it has declined to 2.5 percent.

What is attractive about depressants? Most Central Nervous System depressants act on the brain by increasing activity of gamma-aminobutyric acid (GABA), a chemical that inhibits or slows brain activity. This causes a drowsy calming effect that makes the medicine helpful in treating anxiety and sleep disorders.

The majority of teens I treated preferred Xanax. Max was fifteen when he was admitted to the hospital. He purchased Xanax from friends who sold part of their prescription for five dollars a pill. If your child has a prescription for anxiety medication, carefully monitor use so they're taken as prescribed and not being sold. Under medical supervision these medications are effective but have a high potential for abuse.

CHAPTER TEN

Hallucinogens and Dissociative Drugs[39]

Hallucinogens and dissociative drugs do exactly what the name implies—cause hallucinations or profound distortions in a person's perceptions of reality. They are commonly divided into two categories: classic hallucinogens and dissociative drugs. When under the influence of either type of drug, within twenty to ninety minutes people often report rapid, intense emotional swings and seeing images, hearing sounds, and feeling sensations that seem real but are not. These effects can last as long as twelve hours.

Hallucinogen experiences can be unpredictable and may vary with the amount ingested, coupled with the user's personality, mood, expectations, and surroundings. The effects can instigate a type of psychosis called "trips," where the more unpleasant experiences are called "bad trips."

CLASSIC HALLUCINOGENS

LSD, also called acid, is known by many as the drug of choice by killer Charles Manson and his followers. It is one of the most potent mood and perception altering hallucinogenic drugs. It is a clear or white, odorless, water-soluble material synthesized from lysergic acid. LSD is initially created in crystalline form, which can then be used to make tablets known as microdots, or thin squares of gelatin called window panes. It can be diluted with water or alcohol and sold in liquid form. About 2 percent of tenth graders and 4 percent of seniors use LSD.

The most common form is LSD-soaked paper punched into individual one-quarter-inch squares, known as blotters. LSD is measured in micrograms, or 1/1,000,000 of a gram. A common dose is 50 to 150 micrograms, but I've had adult patients take up to 400 micrograms.

Short-term effects include increased blood pressure, heart rate, and body temperature, along with dizziness and sleeplessness, a loss of appetite, dry mouth, and sweating. Some users experience numbness, weakness, tremors, impulsiveness, and rapid emotional shifts that can range from fear to euphoria. The unpredictability of this drug is what makes it so dangerous for users.

Twenty-nine percent of seniors say LSD is either fairly easy or very easy to get. Sixteen percent of tenth graders and 7 percent of eighth graders say the same.

Psilocybin, known as magic mushrooms, is extracted from certain types of mushrooms found in tropical and sub-tropical regions of South America, Mexico, and the United States. Psilocybin can either be dried or fresh and eaten raw, mixed with food, or brewed into a tea and produces similar effects to LSD. Short-term effects include nervousness, paranoia, and a state of panic.

Peyote (mescaline) is a small cactus that is primarily mescaline. The top or crown of the cactus has disc-shaped buttons that are cut out, dried, and usually chewed or soaked in water to produce an intoxicating drink. It produces cognitive, emotional, and perceptual experiences that vary widely among users.

Short-term effects include increased body temperature and heart rate, uncoordinated movements, profound sweating, and extreme flushing.

DMT is a powerful hallucinogenic chemical found in some Amazonian plant species, but synthetic DMT is created as a white crystalline powder that is vaporized or smoked in a pipe. Short-term effects include increased heart rate, agitation, and hallucinations frequently involving radically altered environments as well as body and spatial distortions.

DISSOCIATIVE DRUGS

Dissociative drugs create a sense of separation from reality. They can produce visual and auditory distortions and a sense of floating and feeling detached from reality. Prolonged use may cause anxiety, memory loss, and impaired motor function, including body tremors and numbness.

Low to moderate doses produce numbness, disorientation, confusion, dizziness, vomiting, hallucinations, and a detachment from self and the environment. High doses can cause hallucinations, memory loss, and psychological distress, including feelings of extreme panic, fear, anxiety, paranoia, invulnerability, exaggerated strength, and aggression.

PCP was developed in the 1950s as a general anesthetic for surgery, but it has since been sold as a liquid or powder that is snorted, smoked, injected, or swallowed. It's sometimes smoked after being sprinkled on marijuana, tobacco, or parsley. The percent of seniors using PCP has remained stable at 1 percent since 2002.

Ketamine is known as K, Special K, or cat. It's a dissociative drug used as an anesthetic for humans and animals. Ketamine is often sold on the street and diverted from veterinary offices. It's usually evaporated to form a powder that can be snorted or compressed into pills for illicit use.

DXM (dextromethorphan) is known as "robo," and teens call using it "robo tripping." Street names include purple drank, lean, and Triple Cs. It's a cough suppressant and expectorant ingredient in some over-the-counter cold and cough medicines. The most common source of abused DXM is extra-strength cough syrup obtained at any pharmacy. In large doses it causes confusion, dizziness, slurred speech, hallucinations, and impaired vision. It's the most abused dissociative used by teens. Eighth grade students use OTC cough/cold medicines at higher rates than tenth and twelfth graders, most likely due to easy availability.

Salvia divinorum is a psychoactive plant ingested by chewing fresh leaves or by drinking its extracted juices. The dried leaves of salvia can be smoked or vaporized and inhaled. With use, the drug changes brain chemistry and causes hallucinations that last less than thirty minutes but can be intense.

While most of these drugs are not widely used by today's adolescents, it's helpful to be aware of them as they may surface at any time.

CHAPTER ELEVEN

Inhalants[40]

Nora Volkow, the director of the National Institute on Drug Abuse, observes that "although many parents are appropriately concerned about illicit drugs such as marijuana, cocaine and LSD, they often ignore the dangers posed to their children from common household products that contain volatile solvents or aerosols. Products such as glues, nail polish remover, lighter fluid, spray paints… are widely available yet far from innocuous."

Inhalants rank as one of the most common and accessible substances that produce chemical vapors that can be inhaled to induce a psychoactive, mind-altering effect. They include substances whose main common characteristic is that they are usually inhaled.

Volatile solvents are "found in a multitude of inexpensive, easily available products used for common household and industrial purposes. These include paint thinners and removers, dry-cleaning fluids, degreasers, gasoline, glues, correction fluids and felt-tip markers."

Aerosols are sprays that contain propellants and solvents, and include spray paints, deodorant and hair sprays, vegetable oil sprays, and fabric protective sprays.

Gases include medical anesthetics and everyday household products. Medical anesthetics are ether, chloroform, halothane, and nitrous oxide (commonly called laughing gas). Nitrous oxide is the most abused of these gases and is found in whipped cream dispensers.

Nitrous oxide canisters are easily obtained from the Internet in boxes of fifty or more canisters. Teens often use multiple boxes in one sitting. I've had patients using 100 or more canisters in a single sitting. Small canisters of nitrous oxide are called "whippits." A "cracker" is a small metal object used to open the canisters.

Inhalant abusers will use any available substance to find a high. However, effects produced by individual inhalants vary and some users will go out of their way to obtain their favorite inhalant. These substances can be inhaled through the nose or mouth in different ways:

- sniffing or snorting fumes from containers;
- spraying aerosols directly into the nose or mouth;
- "bagging," which means sniffing or inhaling fumes from inside a plastic or paper bag;
- "huffing" from an inhalant-soaked rag stuffed in
- the mouth; and
- inhaling from balloons filled with nitrous oxide.

Inhalants "are absorbed rapidly into the bloodstream through the lungs and are quickly distributed to the brain and other organs. Within seconds of inhalation, the user experiences intoxication along with other effects similar to those produced by alcohol. Because intoxication lasts only a few minutes, abusers frequently seek to prolong the high by inhaling repeatedly over the course of several hours, which is a very dangerous practice."

Inhalants can produce irregular and rapid heart rhythms and may lead to fatal heart failure within minutes of prolonged sniffing. This syndrome, known as sudden sniffing death, can result from a single session of inhalant use by an otherwise healthy young person, making it deadlier than users might think.

The National Institute on Drug abuse names the following warning signs of inhalant use:

- chemical odors on breath or clothing;
- paint or other stains on face, hands, or clothes;
- hidden empty spray paint or solvent containers and
- chemical-soaked rags/clothing;
- drunk or disoriented appearance;
- slurred speech;
- nausea or loss of appetite; and
- inattentiveness, lack of coordination, irritability, and depression.

Adolescents tend to use inhalants in the lower grades. About 5 percent of eighth graders, 3 percent of tenth graders, and less than 2 percent of seniors use them. Also, less than half of eighth graders believe *regular inhalant use* is a great risk. Some students experiment with inhalants prior to moving to other drugs later in their teen years.

Chapter Twelve

MDMA (Ecstasy/Molly)[41]

MDMA is a synthetic drug that alters one's mood and awareness of surrounding objects and environment. It is similar to both stimulants and hallucinogens in that it produces feelings of increased energy, pleasure, emotional warmth, and distorted sensory and time perception. It first became popularized in the nightclub scene and at all-night dance parties called raves, but the drug has since found its way into the hands of a broader range of users who more commonly call the drug Ecstasy or Molly.

MDMA is usually taken in capsule or tablet form, although some teens snort the capsule's powder. The popular nickname Molly, slang for *molecular*, refers to the crystalline powder form of MDMA, usually sold in capsules. It's often taken in combination with alcohol or marijuana.

What makes MDMA unique is its ability to increase activity in three brain neurotransmitters: dopamine, norepinephrine, and serotonin. The increase in dopamine produces higher energy/activity and acts in the reward system to reinforce behaviors. The boost of norepinephrine increases heart rate and blood pressure, which can be risky for people with heart and blood vessel problems. Serotonin affects mood, appetite, sleep, and other basic functions. It also triggers hormones that affect sexual arousal and trust. The release of large amounts of serotonin likely cause the emotional closeness, elevated mood, and empathy felt when using MDMA.

The effects can last anywhere between three to six hours, although many users take a second dose as the effects of the first dose begin to fade. Over the course of the week following moderate use of MDMA, a person may experience irritability, impulsiveness, aggression, depression, sleep problems, anxiety, memory and attention problems, and decreased appetite. These are some of the symptoms you should look for if you suspect MDMA use in your family.

Luckily, MDMA use has declined since 2000 when over 8 percent of seniors used it. Today, about 2 percent of students in eighth, tenth and twelfth grades use MDMA, but we hope with growing awareness of the risks involved that use will continue to decrease.

CHAPTER THIRTEEN

Process Disorders

How do you know if your teen has a substance problem? The inability to control substance use despite negative consequences is a classic definition of a severe substance use disorder. But substances aren't the only thing afflicting adolescents. Another dangerous behavior is invading the adolescent population: process disorders. These are compulsive behaviors often accompanying alcohol and drug disorders, though not always. Examples include sex, shopping and spending, gambling, gaming, eating disorders, self-harm, and cell phone use.

The process disorders I frequently saw among adolescents were eating disorders, self-injury, and to a lesser extent gaming. Patients with eating disorders were mostly females, while males presented with gaming disorders.

These behaviors can evolve without your child using alcohol or drugs, but it's not uncommon to have both a substance use disorder combined with a process disorder. For example, teens might be smoking marijuana and engaging in self-harm by cutting or burning themselves. When both disorders are present, treatment becomes more complicated.

Self-Harm[42] refers to injuring yourself on purpose and can be a symptom of extreme emotional distress. Unfortunately, this act is becoming increasingly common in teens.

Research from the Centers for Disease Control shows that up to 30 percent of teenage girls say they have intentionally injured themselves and about one in ten boys engaged in self-inflicted injury. Combined, nearly 18 percent of teens have used methods of self-harm, the most prevalent method being cutting. As a result, this trend has become an ongoing danger.

Beth was admitted to the psychiatric unit with a history of cutting beginning at age ten. She smoked marijuana multiple times a day and showed traits of Borderline Personality Disorder (BPD). BPD involves difficulties regulating emotion, which means that people who experience BPD feel emotions intensely and for extended periods of time.

Like most self-harming teens, Beth concealed her cutting for years. She cut in areas unnoticed by her parents, such as her thighs, upper legs, and arms. This coping skill helped relieve intense feelings of anxiety and guilt, though it left physical and emotional scarring. Without access to marijuana, Beth's self-harm increased while she was hospitalized as she found staples or pens and made superficial scratches on her arms.

If your child is self-harming, you may not understand it, or you might ask, "Why would anyone, especially my child, intentionally harm themselves?"

Self-harm is a coping skill to manage intolerable feelings like anger, shame, grief, guilt, or self-loathing. It's a desperate attempt to gain control over these emotions. Also, some teens self-harm because they want to punish themselves for what they perceive as their faults or flaws.

While some teens cut with a knife or other sharp object, other methods of self-harm include the following:

- scratching or biting the skin;
- burning the skin with matches, cigarettes, or hot, sharp objects;
- hitting or punching themselves or the walls;
- piercing their skin with sharp objects; and
- banging their head or body against walls and hard objects.

Teens will go to great lengths to hide their wounds and self-harming instruments. Here are some warning signs:

- scars or scabs;
- unexplained cuts, scratches, bruises, or other wounds often found on wrists, arms, and thighs;
- keeping sharp objects on hand;
- wearing clothes that cover up the skin, such as long sleeves or pants in hot weather;
- impulsive and unstable behavior;
- expressing feelings of hopelessness or worthlessness;
- difficulties with relationships;
- blood stains on bedding, clothing, towels, or tissues;

- having sharp objects in their possession, including razors, scissors, and needles;

- spending long periods of time alone, often in the bathroom or bedroom; and

- avoiding situations where they need to reveal skin, such as swimming.

Therapies for self-harm include Cognitive Behavioral Therapy (CBT) and Dialectical Behavioral Therapy (DBT). Your child can learn to practice safe, effective coping skills in DBT groups. The success of such treatment, however, depends on a willingness to practice these coping skills. Beth attended numerous DBP training classes. She knew all the DBT acronyms and skills but never practiced them or committed to using them when needed. As a result, she was setting herself up for failure.

It's fairly easy to keep patients away from alcohol and drugs in an acute hospital setting. It's more challenging in residential and outpatient programs. For example, if there is a history of marijuana use and self-harm like cutting, controlling the cutting becomes a challenge.

Another patient named Julie, much like Beth, smoked marijuana multiple times a day and self-harmed to manage anxiety. Because she was in a psychiatric hospital, her access to marijuana was denied. When her anxiety spiked, her self-harm increased because she didn't access her other coping skill of smoking marijuana. That's the challenge with adolescents diagnosed with a substance use disorder and a process disorder like self-harm or an eating disorder. Both disorders are coping skills and when one skill is curtailed, the other may increase.

The Self Abuse Finally Ends (S.A.F.E) website offers information and resources you may find helpful. There is information for family members and intervention tips. The website is https://selfinjury.com

Eating Disorders. The American Academy of Child and Adolescent Psychiatry believes that the two primary psychiatric eating disorders, anorexia nervosa and bulimia, are on the rise among teenage girls. While these two eating disorders also occur in boys, it's less often.[43]

A teenager with anorexia nervosa is typically female, a perfectionist, and a high achiever in school. At the same time, she suffers from low self-esteem, irrationally believing she is fat regardless of how thin she becomes. Desperately searching for a feeling of mastery over her life, a teenager with anorexia nervosa experiences a sense of control only when she says no to the normal food demands of her body. In a relentless pursuit to be thin, the girl starves herself.[44]

Symptoms of bulimia are different as the patient binges on large quantities of high-caloric food followed by purging the body of dreaded calories by self-induced vomiting, extreme exercise, or laxatives. The binges may alternate with severe diets, resulting in dramatic weight fluctuations. Teenagers may try to hide the signs of throwing up by running water while spending long periods of time in the bathroom.[45]

Treatment for eating disorders usually requires a team approach, including individual therapy, family therapy, working with a primary care physician, seeking out a nutritionist, and medication. Parents who notice symptoms in their teenagers should ask their family physician or pediatrician for a referral to a child and adolescent psychiatrist.[46]

Eating Disorders[47] often go unnoticed, and "most parents do not realize how common teen eating disorders are. In most cases, the onset of eating disorders occurs in adolescence or early adulthood." What's worse is that these disorders can be deadly. Every 62 minutes, a person dies from an eating disorder.

How can you detect if your child has an eating disorder? You'll notice that your adolescent tends to be moody, anxious, and/or depressed. Most adolescents suffering from eating disorders will deny that they have a problem. In many cases, they'll blame everything but their relationship with food.

Here are the behavioral signs and physical symptoms to look for:

Behavioral Signs

(1) making excuses to avoid eating;

(2) always being on a diet, even when not needed;

(3) over-exercising, and obsessed with exercise to lose weight;

(4) secretly storing food or eating alone, particularly at night;

(5) a distorted body image;

(6) compulsive use of laxatives, diet pills and weight-loss aids;

(7) an intense, obsessive focus on calories and caloric intake;

(8) an unwillingness to discuss weight gains or weight loss;

(9) resistance to joining social situations where eating is expected;

(10) extended bathroom use during or right after meals.

Similar behavioral signs can appear in adolescent girls and boys going through normal childhood development. Still, when teens repeatedly exhibit a number of these behaviors, the parents should investigate further.

PHYSICAL SYMPTOMS

(1) unhealthy loss or gain of weight;

(2) repeated weight cycling, going up and down;

(3) constipation or vomiting;

(4) skin rash or dry skin;

(5) erosion of tooth enamel, dental cavities;

(6) loss of hair and/or nail quality;

(7) obvious signs of exhaustion or insomnia;

(8) irregular menstruation or absence of menstruation;

(9) easily bruised or more prone to physical injury;

(10) cold sensitivity.

One referral site for eating disorders is ED Referral. It offers search programs and the ability to identify specific co-occurring issues like addiction. Also, you can search for programs by insurance. Under the Find Help tab, selecting "Only for Treatment

Centers" brings a list of programs where you can select a program and view the program's site. The website is www.EDReferral.com.

Gaming[48] has been classified as a disorder by the World Health Organization (WHO). WHO defines a gaming disorder as "a pattern of gaming behavior (digital-gaming or video-gaming) characterized by impaired control over gaming, increasing priority given to gaming over other activities to the extent that gaming takes precedence over other interests and daily activities, and continuation or escalation of gaming despite the occurrence of negative consequences."

Tommy was introduced to video games at age seven. Fast-forward nine years when he was admitted to the hospital at age sixteen as a result of playing video games multiple times a day. His gaming interfered with school assignments and his grades were falling. He became angry and argumentative when his mother confronted him and placed limits on his gaming. Tommy violated every limit and when his mother removed his game console, he stole his brother's. It soon became apparent that Tommy needed treatment to help control his gaming addiction.

If you suspect your child is becoming addicted to gaming, look for the following symptoms:

(1) preoccupation with internet gaming,

(2) video game withdrawal like sadness, anxiety, and irritability if games are removed,

(3) an ongoing need to spend more time gaming,

(4) inability to reduce time spent playing games and unsuccessful attempts to quit playing,

(5) loss of interest in other activities they previously enjoyed,

(6) playing despite significant problems caused by gaming,

(7) lying to family members/others about the amount of time spent on computer gaming,

(8) using video gaming to self-medicate moods,

(9) forgoing basic needs, such as eating, sleeping, and hygiene while playing,

(10) social isolation as a result of gaming, and

(11) losing a job, losing a relationship, or doing poorly in school as a result of gaming.

Cell phone[49] usage is the latest addiction that plagues both youths and adults. Does your child's cell phone usage seem excessive? Do you argue about the time they spend on their phone? Cell phone addiction is often an important issue parents face.

Your child's obsession with their cell phone goes well beyond texting and talking. As basically a mini-computer, it includes apps, games, and, in particular, social media. For teens, cell phones have become a way to comment and criticize, approve and admire, all at the touch of a finger and with little to no accountability.

Your child's brain reacts to the cell phone as if it were a drug. Studies show both the phone ringing and the alert of a new text cause the brain to release dopamine, which is a common reaction during drug use. Also, your child may experience a drug-like withdrawal process when not allowed to use their cell phone, including increased aggression in connection to controlling the cell phone.

We know that driving under the influence of a substance is dangerous. Distractions while driving can be just as dangerous, especially for teens who are inexperienced drivers.

The National Highway Transportation Safety Administration (NHTSA)[50] believes one third of teens text on their cell phone while driving. Furthermore, simply dialing a phone number while driving increases a teen's risk of crashing by six times and texting increases the risk by twenty-three times. The NHTSA warns that "taking eyes off the road for even five seconds could cost a life."

It's important that you set consequences for any distracted driving. For example, you might suspend their driving privileges or limiting the hours they can drive. If necessary, you can place limits on their cell phone use.

You may want to limit the number of passengers in your teen's car. The NHTSA found that teens are more likely to engage in risky behaviors when passengers are present. In one study, "teen drivers were two-and-a-half times more likely to engage in one or more potentially risky behaviors when driving with one teenage peer, compared to when driving alone."[51] Also, the risk of a teen being involved in a fatal crash increases with the number of passengers. You should establish rules on who can ride with your child and how many people can be in the car.

If your child's cell phone use worries you, you are not alone. Fifty-nine percent of parents feel their teens are addicted to their mobile devices. Here are some other alarming statistics:

- 78 percent of teens check their mobile devices at least hourly.

- 72 percent of teens feel an urgent need to immediately respond to texts.

- 77 percent of parents feel their teens get distracted by their cell phones.

- 30 percent of both teens and parents claim to argue about mobile devices and cell phones on a daily basis.

- 44 percent of teens use their mobile devices at the dinner table.

Cell phone addiction drains one's attention, and teens' intense focus on cell phones distracts them from everyday life. They are not present in their own lives. Once cell phone addiction sets in, behaviors can rapidly change. Grades at school can drop and participation in extracurricular activities can diminish. Did you know that 61 percent of kids say smartphone use has had a negative impact on their schoolwork?

If you are concerned about your child's excessive cell phone use, you can set boundaries and restrict privileges. For example, you can impose strict data limits to control their phone use. You can install password activated programs that shut off cell phones at designated times. Your cell phone provider can help you with this. If boundaries aren't working, professional help might be warranted.

How do you know if your teen needs a break from the device? When a teen loses their cell phone privileges, they often feel and act like it's the end of the world, resulting in an extreme reaction. Luckily, such dramatic responses pass more quickly than you would expect in the majority of cases.[52]

Your teen might be using alcohol or drugs *and* be engaged in a process disorder. If you suspect this is the case, you should notify those doing the substance use assessment. Treating one disorder (alcohol/drugs) without treating the other disorder (process disorder) is a blueprint for failure. Unless both disorders are treated, success in curtailing one might lead to an increased use of the other.

Chapter Fourteen

Principles of Adolescent Substance Abuse Treatment[53]

Searching for your child's treatment program can be exhausting and frustrating. Friends and relatives offer well-meaning advice when all you really want is effective treatment for your child. Fortunately, these principles from the National Institute on Drug Abuse can guide your search:

Adolescent substance abuse needs to be identified and addressed as soon as possible. Drugs can have long-lasting effects on the developing brain and may interfere with family, positive peer relationships, and school performance. Most adults who develop a substance use disorder report having started drug use in adolescence or young adulthood, so it's important to identify and intervene early.

Adolescents can benefit from a drug abuse intervention even if they are not addicted to a drug. Substance use disorders range from problematic use to addiction and can be treated successfully at any stage, and at any age. For young people, any drug use (even if it seems like only "experimentation") is cause for concern, as it exposes them to dangers from the drug and associated risky behaviors, which may lead to more drug use in the future. Parents should monitor their child and not underestimate the significance of what may appear as isolated instances of drug taking.

Routine annual medical visits are an opportunity to ask adolescents about drug use. Standardized screening tools are available to help pediatricians, dentists, emergency room doctors, psychiatrists, and other clinicians determine an adolescent's level of involvement (if any) in tobacco, alcohol, and illicit and nonmedical prescription drug use. When an adolescent reports substance use, the health care provider can assess its severity and either provide an onsite brief intervention or refer the teen to a substance abuse treatment program. You should ask your child's pediatrician to perform a screen for substance use during any routine examination.

Legal interventions and sanctions or family pressure may play an important role in getting adolescents to enter, stay in, and complete treatment. Adolescents with substance use disorders rarely feel they need treatment and almost never seek it on their own. *Research shows that treatment can work even if it's mandated or entered into unwillingly.* Outcome studies from court-ordered treatment placements show mandated treatment can work. "Most studies suggest that outcomes for those who are legally pressured to enter treatment are as good as or better than outcomes for those who entered treatment without legal pressure."[54]

Substance use disorder treatment should be tailored to the unique needs of the adolescent. Treatment planning begins with a comprehensive assessment to identify the person's strengths and weaknesses that need to be addressed. Appropriate treatment considers an adolescent's level of psychological development, gender, relations with family and peers, how well he or she is doing in school, the larger community, cultural and ethnic factors, and any special physical or behavioral issues.

Treatment should address the needs of the whole person, rather than just focusing on his or her drug use. The best approach to treatment includes supporting the adolescent's larger life needs, such as those related to medical, psychological, and social well-being, as well as housing, school, transportation, and legal services. Failing to address such needs simultaneously could sabotage the adolescent's treatment success.

Behavioral therapies are effective in addressing adolescent drug use. Behavioral therapies, delivered by trained clinicians, help an adolescent stay off drugs by strengthening his or her motivation to change. This can be done by providing incentives for abstinence, building skills to resist and refuse substances and deal with triggers or cravings, replacing drug use with constructive and rewarding activities, improving problem-solving skills, and facilitating better interpersonal relationships.

Families and the community are important aspects of treatment. The support of family members is important for an adolescent's recovery. Several evidence-based interventions for adolescent drug abuse seek to strengthen family relationships by improving communication and improving family members' ability to support abstinence from drugs. In addition, members of the community (such as school counselors, parents, peers, and mentors) can encourage young people who need help to get into treatment—and support them along the way.

Effectively treating substance use disorders in adolescents requires also identifying and treating any other mental health conditions they may have. Adolescents who abuse drugs frequently suffer from other conditions including depression, anxiety disorders, attention-deficit hyperactivity disorder, oppositional defiant disorder, and conduct problems. Adolescents who abuse drugs should be screened for other psychiatric disorders. Treatment for these problems should be integrated with the treatment plan for a substance use disorder.

Sensitive issues such as violence and child abuse or risk of suicide should be identified and addressed. Many adolescents who abuse drugs have a history of physical, emotional, and/or sexual abuse or other trauma. The use of alcohol or drugs can be a coping skill to deal with these intolerable emotions that need to be addressed in substance abuse treatment.

It's important to monitor drug use during treatment. Adolescents recovering from substance use disorders may experience relapse, or a return to drug use. Triggers associated with relapse vary and can include mental stress and social situations linked with prior drug use. It's important to identify a return to drug use early before an undetected relapse progresses to more serious consequences. A relapse signals the need for more treatment or a need to adjust the individual's treatment plan to better meet his or her needs.

Staying in treatment for an adequate period of time and continuity of care afterward are important. The minimal length of drug treatment depends on the type and extent of the adolescent's problems, *but studies show outcomes are better when a person stays in treatment for three months or more.* Because relapses often occur, more than one episode of treatment may be necessary. Many adolescents also benefit from continuing care following treatment, including drug use monitoring and linking the family to other needed services.

Testing adolescents for sexually transmitted diseases like HIV, as well as hepatitis B and C, is an important part of drug treatment. Adolescents who use drugs—whether injecting or non-injecting—are at increased risk for diseases that are transmitted sexually as well as through the blood. All abused drugs alter judgment and decision making, increasing the likelihood that an adolescent will engage in unprotected sex and other high-risk behaviors.

CHAPTER FIFTEEN

Types of Treatment[55]

How do you find the best program for your child's unique needs? What programs treat mental health and substance abuse? What programs fit your budget? These are important questions that every parent asks when they first face a need for treatment. So where should you begin?

You should start with the treatment team members that performed your child's assessments. This might be the psychiatrist, psychologist, social worker or addictions counselor who completed one of your child's assessments. They're familiar with your child's issues and diagnoses and can recommend the best programs for effective therapy.

Some families employ "educational consultants" who specialize in matching their child's psychological and addiction needs with appropriate treatment programs. Consultants interview members of the treatment team and are familiar with programs around the country. Two educational consultant groups are listed in the closing resources chapter.

Inpatient programs are provided in special units of hospitals or medical clinics, and offer both detoxification and rehabilitation services. People who have a medical disorder or serious medical problems, combined with a substance use disorder, are the ones most likely to receive inpatient treatment. Adolescents may also need the structure of impatient treatment to make sure a full assessment of their substance use and mental disorders can be handled at once. These programs offer comprehensive assessments focusing on medical, psychological, and addictions issues.

Residential programs provide a living environment with treatment services all in one place. Residential programs often have phases of treatment, with different expectations and activities during each phase. For example, an adolescent may be able to have contact with his or her parents but not with friends or with school. This restriction helps the person become part of the treatment community and adjust to the treatment setting to allow them to focus on their current healing. Residential programs are a preferred form of treatment for adolescents diagnosed with severe mental health issues and co-occurring substance abuse.

The Substance Abuse and Mental Health Services Administration (SAMHSA) offers a booklet for families entitled What Is Substance Abuse Treatment? The booklet identifies different treatment approaches:

Partial hospitalization or day treatment takes a less intensive approach than residential care. These programs, located in hospitals or clinics, offer treatment for four to eight hours per day while the patient lives at home. A minimum of three months is advised and it works best for people who have a stable, supportive home environment.

Outpatient and intensive outpatient programs provide treatment at a program site while the patient lives elsewhere, usually at home. Outpatient treatment is offered in a variety of places, like health clinics, community mental health clinics, counselors' offices, hospital clinics, local health department offices, or residential programs with outpatient clinics. While an outpatient program is appropriate for some adolescents, those with more severe alcohol, substance use, process disorders, or psychological issues usually require an inpatient or residential program followed by a step-down outpatient program.

COMMON ELEMENTS

While treatment programs differ, SAMHSA notes most include common elements that benefit all patients:

Assessments: All treatment programs begin with a clinical assessment of a person's individual treatment needs. This initial assessment shapes an effective treatment plan catered to each person.

Medical Care: Hospital and residential programs provide medical care under the direction of a physician, usually a psychiatrist. This includes medication management and crisis management of medical and psychiatric issues.

Treatment Plan: The treatment team, along with the person in treatment, develops a treatment plan based on the assessment. This written guide for treatment includes the person's goals, treatment activities designed to help him or her meet those goals, ways to tell whether a goal has been met, and a timeframe for meeting goals. It may be adjusted over time to meet changing needs in order to ensure that it stays relevant to the patient's growth.

Discharge Planning: As discharge nears, the treatment team, adolescent, and family prepare a discharge plan. This includes follow-up medications and psychological care, a relapse prevention plan, academic or vocational plans, and family re-orientation plans. Prior to discharge you should arrange medical and psychological follow-up appointments.

Group and Individual Counseling: Individual counseling is different in each program. However, it usually focuses on motivating your teen to stop using drugs or alcohol and addresses the psychological issues driving substance use. Treatment then shifts to staying drug and alcohol free. It's interesting to note that teens usually respond to a neuroscience approach. Because substance use impacts the entire family, most programs offer family therapy sessions.

Wilderness Programs: For the more defiant user, these programs address adolescents who are reluctant to enter substance abuse/mental health residential treatment programs. Participants are exposed to therapy in a natural environment (the wilderness), where addictions issues, responsibility, self-esteem, and coping skills are emphasized. These programs can motivate and prepare a resistant teen for residential treatment. The National Association of Therapeutic Schools and Programs offers parents resources and a guide to finding these programs.

The National Institute on Drug Abuse (NIDA) believes that "finding the right treatment for a person's specific needs is critical. Drug abuse treatment is not 'one size fits all.' Treatment outcomes depend on the extent and nature of the person's problems, appropriateness of treatment, availability of additional services and quality of interaction between the person and his or her treatment providers."[56] NIDA suggests asking the following questions when searching for a treatment program:[57]

Does the program use treatments backed by scientific evidence? Effective drug abuse treatments include behavioral therapy, medications, or, ideally, a combination of both. Behavioral therapies vary in focus and may involve:

- addressing a patient's motivation to change;

- providing incentives to stop taking drugs;

- building skills to resist drug use;

- replacing drug-using activities with constructive and rewarding activities;

- improving problem-solving skills; and

- building better personal relationships.

Examples of behavioral therapies include:

Cognitive Behavioral Therapy. CBT seeks to help patients recognize, avoid, and cope with stressful or emotional situations in which they are most likely to abuse drugs.

Motivational Incentives. Incentives apply positive reinforcements, such as providing rewards or privileges, to encourage a patient to remain drug free, to participate in counseling sessions, or to take treatment medications as prescribed.

Motivational Interviewing. This form of self-reflection offers strategies to encourage rapid and self-driven behavioral change to stop drug use and help a patient enter treatment.

Group Therapy. There is power in numbers. Group therapy helps patients face their drug abuse realistically, come to terms with its harmful consequences, and boost their motivation to stay drug free by connecting with others who share in their common experience.

Does the program tailor treatment to the needs of each patient? No single treatment is right for everyone. The best treatment addresses a person's various needs, not just his or her drug abuse. The best programs provide a combination of therapies and other services to meet a patient's broader needs.

Does the program adapt treatment as the patient's needs change? Individual treatment and service plans must be addressed and modified as needed to meet changing needs. A person in treatment may require varying combinations of services during its course, including ongoing assessment.

Is the duration of treatment sufficient? Remaining in treatment for the right period of time is critical. Appropriate time in treatment depends on the type and degree of a person's problems and needs. Longer treatment times result in better outcomes.

FURTHER QUESTIONS TO ASK

When talking with potential treatment programs, the following questions may be helpful as you plan the scope of treatment and what fits your needs and budget:

- How much does the program cost and are payment options available?

- What's the ratio of staff to patients?

- How many times a week will my child meet with a psychiatrist?

- How many times will my child meet with an addictions counselor and other clinicians?

- What types of therapy groups are offered and how often do they meet?

- Do you offer family therapy sessions? How often?

- Do you offer support groups like AA and NA? If so, how often?

- What's the average age of teens in the program?

- What's the ratio of males to females in the program?

- What's the average length of stay?

- What items are prohibited when my child enters the program?

- Can my child have a phone? A laptop? An eReader?

- What's the procedure for discharge planning?

- Do you have statistics on relapse rates for discharged patients?

- What extracurricular activities do you offer?

- Will I be able to visit my child? If so, how often?

- Do you offer a family orientation program?

The more questions you ask, the better informed you will be. And the more informed you are, the better equipped you'll be to help your child break the bonds of addiction.

CHAPTER SIXTEEN

Evidence-Based Approaches to Treating Adolescent Substance Use Disorders[58]

Research evidence continually supports the effectiveness of various substance abuse treatment approaches for adolescents. While most treatments have been tested for twelve to sixteen weeks, some adolescents require longer treatment to reach optimal results. The ideal length of treatment time is made on a case-by-case basis.

BEHAVIORAL APPROACHES

Behavioral interventions help adolescents actively participate in their recovery from drug abuse and addiction, while reinforcing their ability to resist drug use. Using these approaches, therapists may provide incentives to remain abstinent, modify attitudes and behaviors related to drug use, assist families in improving their communication and overall interactions, and increase life skills to handle stressful circumstances with alternative coping methods.

Adolescent Community Reinforcement Approach (A-CRA) "seeks to help adolescents achieve and maintain abstinence from drugs by replacing influences in their lives that had reinforced substance use with healthier family, social, and educational or vocational reinforcers...The therapist chooses from among 17 A-CRA procedures to address problem-solving, coping, and communication skills and to encourage active participation in constructive social and recreational activities."

Cognitive-Behavioral Therapy (CBT) is based on the theory that learning processes play a critical role in the development of a problem behavior like drug abuse. A core element of CBT teaches participants how to anticipate problems then helps them develop effective, healthy coping strategies. In CBT, adolescents explore the positive and negative consequences of using drugs, then learn to monitor their feelings and thoughts. This helps them recognize distorted thinking patterns and cues that trigger their substance abuse, identify and anticipate high-risk situations, and apply an array of newly developed self-control skills.

The Contingency Management (CM) approach provides adolescents with an opportunity to earn low-cost incentives such as prizes or cash vouchers in exchange for participating in drug treatment, achieving important goals of treatment, and not using drugs. The goal of CM is to weaken the influence of reinforcement derived from drug use and to substitute it with reinforcement derived from healthier activities and drug abstinence.

Motivational Enhancement Therapy (MET) helps reticent adolescents resolve their ambivalence about engaging in treatment or quitting their drug use. It typically includes an initial assessment of the adolescent's motivation to participate in treatment, followed by one of three individual sessions in which a therapist helps the patient develop a desire to participate in treatment by providing non-confrontational feedback. While it's not as effective as other treatments, MET appeals to users who are reluctant to get help. It is typically not recommended as a standalone treatment for adolescents with substance use disorders, but is used to motivate them to participate in other types of treatment.

Twelve-Step Facilitation Therapy is designed to encourage an adolescent with a drug abuse problem to become affiliated and actively involved in a successful twelve-step program like Alcoholics Anonymous (AA) or Narcotics Anonymous (NA). Such programs stress the participant's acceptance that life has become unmanageable, that abstinence from drug use is needed, and that willpower alone cannot overcome the problem. It's important that adolescents involved in these groups attend adolescent-only groups and not adult groups.

FAMILY-BASED APPROACHES

Family-based approaches highlight the need to engage the entire family, including parents, siblings, and sometimes peers, in the adolescent's treatment. Involving those closest to the patient can be particularly important, as the adolescent will often be living with at least one parent and be subject to the parent's controls, rules, and/or support. Also, these approaches address multiple mental and emotional issues in addition to the adolescent's substance problem.

Brief Strategic Family Therapy (BSFT) is based on a family systems approach to treatment, in which one member's problem behaviors seem to stem from unhealthy family interactions. Over the course of twelve to sixteen sessions, the BSFT counselor establishes a relationship with each family member, observes how the members behave with one another, and assists the family in changing negative interaction patterns that negatively impact the patient.

Family Behavior Therapy (FBT) is one that "combines behavioral contracting with contingency management to address not only substance abuse but other behavioral problems as well. The adolescent and at least one parent participate in treatment planning and choose specific interventions from a menu of evidence-based treatment options."

Multidimensional Family Therapy (MDFT) is a comprehensive family and community-based treatment for substance abusing adolescents and those at risk of behavior problems, such as conduct disorder and delinquency. The aim of MDFT is to foster family competency and collaboration with other systems like school and juvenile justice.

Multisystemic Therapy (MST) is a comprehensive and intensive family and community-based treatment that has been shown to be effective even with adolescents whose substance abuse problems are severe and with those who engage in delinquent or violent behavior. In MST, the adolescent's substance abuse is viewed in terms of the patient's characteristics that give the user a favorable attitude toward drug use, and it also assesses the attitudes of his family, peers, school, and neighborhood.

RECOVERY SUPPORT SERVICES

Recovery support groups reinforce gains made in treatment to encourage continued recovery. Recovering adolescents may benefit from recovery support services, which include continuing care, mutual help groups (such as twelve-step programs), peer recovery support services, and recovery high schools. These services are not substitutes for treatment, rather they complement it. Note that the existing research evidence supporting these approaches (with the exception of Assertive Continuing Care) is preliminary.

Assertive Continuing Care (ACC) is a home-based continuing care approach delivered by trained clinicians to prevent relapse, and it is typically used after an adolescent completes therapy. ACC aims to help adolescents and their caregivers acquire the skills to engage in positive social activities that will lead to drug-free maintenance.

Mutual Help Groups are support groups such as the twelve-step programs like Alcoholics Anonymous (AA) and Narcotic Anonymous (NA). They provide ongoing support for people with addictions to alcohol and drugs, respectively, free of charge and in a community setting. Participants meet in a group with others in recovery once a week or more, sharing their experiences and offering mutual support. It's important that adolescents attend groups intended for teens and not adults.

Recovery High Schools are schools specifically designed for students recovering from substance abuse issues. They are typically part of another school or set of alternative school programs within the public school system, but recovery school students are generally separated from mainstream students by means of scheduling and physical barriers. Peer support programs allow adolescents newly in recovery to be surrounded by a similar-minded group supportive of recovery efforts and attitudes.

CHAPTER SEVENTEEN

Resources

EDUCATION CONSULTANTS AND WILDERNESS PROGRAMS

ECS (Therapeutic and Educational Placement Options) is a national firm that offers advice, guidance, and advocacy to families seeking change. Their website links to ECS publications including an article on questions to ask an education consultant. www.ecs4families.org

Independent Educational Consultants Association recognizes consultants specializing in helping families with troubled teens. Consultants are experienced in crisis intervention, dealing with oppositional behaviors, and other emotional/behavioral difficulties, and finding the most suitable solutions. Their site covers topics one might ask, such as "What is an independent education consultant?" and "How can an IECA member consultant help your family?" There's a link to "therapeutic needs" and consultants who specialize in helping families with troubled teens. https://www.iecaonline.com

National Association of Therapeutic Schools and Programs was created in January of 1999 to serve as a national resource for programs and professionals assisting young people beleaguered by emotional and behavioral difficulties. The association is governed by an elected, volunteer Board of Directors comprised of representatives from the NATSAP membership. Their website has information on finding programs, questions to ask, and financial options. https://natsap.org

MENTAL HEALTH RESOURCES

Substance Abuse and Mental Health Services Administration oversees and administers programs on mental health, drug abuse prevention, and drug treatment. Their website provides resources on substances and treatment, along with publications on mental health and addiction. https://www.samhsa.gov

Substance Abuse and Mental Health Services Helpline is a confidential, free, twenty-four-hour information service for individuals and family members facing mental health and/or substance use disorders. The service provides referrals to local treatment facilities, support groups, and community-based organizations. 1-800-662-HELP (4357)

National Alliance on Mental Health is the nation's largest mental health organization and offers education and advocacy for mental health issues and programs for families. www.nami.org

American Academy of Child and Adolescent Psychiatry offers information for families under links for families and youth, facts for families, and family resources. https://www.aacap.org/

Substance Abuse and Self-Harm Resources

Above the Influence gives facts to teens that help them stand up to negative influences, including the pressure to use drugs and alcohol. www.abovetheinfluence.com

Easy-To-Read Drug Facts is provided by the National Institute on Drug Abuse. The site has pictures and videos on drugs, addiction, treatment, and prevention. The website can read each page out loud. www.easyread.drugabuse.gov

Healthy Children Org is sponsored by the American Academy of Pediatrics and provides resources on substance abuse and treatment. *A Parent's Guide to Teen Parties* and *Drug Abuse Prevention Starts with Parents* is available along with information on substance use under the "Ages of Stages/Teen/Substance Use" tabs. www.healthychildren.org

Mothers Against Drunk Driving includes information on teen drinking prevention and a Power of Parents Handbook under "The Solution" tab. https://www.madd.org

National Institute on Alcohol Abuse and Alcoholism offers resources and education about alcohol use. It includes information on special populations including youth under age twenty-one and a publication for parents entitled "Make a Difference: Talk to Your Child About Alcohol—Parents." https://www.niaaa.nih.gov

National Institute on Drug Abuse provides resources for parents including helpful guides for preventing drug abuse and seeking treatment. www.drugabuse.gov/parents-educators

Partnership for Drug-Free Kids works to reduce substance use among adolescents by supporting families and engaging with teens. The website includes a Parent Blog and one-on-one support with parent "coaches." http://www.drugfree.org

NIDA for Teens has information for teens, parents, and teachers and includes drug facts, activities, and videos. https://teens.drugabuse.gov/

Smokefree.gov includes a "Smokefree Teen" link with articles and tools to help teens quit nicotine use. Teens can sign up for a smoke-free text messaging program that provides 24/7 support to help them quit tobacco use. www.smokefree.gov

Self Abuse Finally Ends (S.A.F.E.) says it "is a nationally recognized treatment approach, professional network and educational resource committed to helping end self-injurious behavior." It offers resources for family members and intervention tips. https://selfinjury.com

Teen-Safe is from the Center for Adolescent Substance Use and Addiction Research (CeASAR) at Boston Children's Hospital. The site has a comprehensive list of resources and parent frequently asked questions. Check out the "Take the Course" link and the view short videos under the teen safe video library. https://teen-safe.org/

U.S. Drug Enforcement Administration enforces controlled substance laws. It provides information on drugs and a publication entitled *Growing Up Free: A Parent's Guide to Prevention* written with the U.S. Department of Education. It's located under the "Resources/Publications/Education and Prevention" tab. www.dea.gov

Centers for Disease Control and Prevention provides information for parents with teens (ages twelve through nineteen). CDC offers information on Raising Healthy Teens (Parenting Tips) and other useful resources. https://www.cdc.gov/parents/teens/index.html

Support Groups

Self-Management and Recovery Training (S.M.A.R.T) is an alternative to twelve-step support groups. Groups are not as widely available as twelve-step groups. S.M.A.R.T. helps individuals focus on motivation, managing emotions, coping with urges to use substances, and building a balanced lifestyle. https://www.smartrecovery.org

Twelve-Step Support Groups are the best-known substance use support groups throughout the world. They include Alcoholics Anonymous (AA) and Narcotics Anonymous (NA), but there are also specialized twelve-step groups on specific disorders like eating disorders. Support groups are member-led to share common experiences and struggles and gain mutual support. They can be an important aspect to substance abuse treatment and recovery. Most adolescent substance abuse treatment programs include a twelve-step group. Following treatment, if your child decides to continue participating in a twelve-step group, it should be an adolescent rather than adult group.

REFERENCES

Notes

1   Johnston, L.D., Miech, R.A., O'Malley, P.M., Bachman, J.G., Schulenberg, J.E., & Patrick, M.E., (2020). Monitoring the Future national survey results on drug use 1975-2019: Overview, key findings on adolescent drug use. Ann Arbor: Institute for Social Research, University of Michigan.

2   Johnson, L.D., Miech, R.A., O'Malley, P.M.,Bachman, J.G., Schulenberg, J.E., & Patrick, M.I. (2019). Monitoring the Future national survey results on drug use 1975-2018: Overview, key findings on adolescent drug use. Ann Arbor: Institute for Social Research, University of Michigan.

3   Centers for Disease Control and Prevention. Substance Use and Sexual Risk Behaviors Among Youth. Retrieved from https://www.cdc.gov/healthyyouth/factsheets/substance_use_fact_sheet-basic.htm

4   NIDA (2014, July1) Drugs, Brains and Behavior: The Science of Addiction. Retrieved from https://www.drugabuse.gov/publications/drugs-brains-behavior-science-addiction

5   NIDA. (2014, January 14). Principles of Adolescent Substance Use Disorder Treatment: A research-based Guide.

Retrieved from https://www.drugabuse.gov/publications/
principles-adolescent-substance-use-disorder-treatment-re-
search-based-guide on 2018 August 15.

6   Ibid.

7   Centers for Substance Abuse Treatment. Enhancing Moti-
vation for Change in Substance Abuse Treatment. Treatment
Improvement Protocol (TIP) Series, No. 35. HHS Publication
No. (SMA) 13-4212. Rockville, MD: Substance Abuse and
Mental Health Services Administration, 1999

8   https://www.drugabuse.gov/publications/media-guide/
science-drug-abuse-addiction-basics

9   NIDA. (2018, July 24). Marijuana: Facts Parents Need to
Know. Retrieved from https://www.drugabuse.gov/publica-
tions/marijuana-facts-parents-need-to-know

10 Underage Drinking. Centers for Disease Control and
Prevention. Retrieved from https://www.cdc.gov/alcohol/fact-
sheets/underage-drinking.htm

11 National Institute on Alcohol Abuse and Alcoholism.
Retrieved from https://www.niaaa.nih.gov/publications/bro-
chures-and-fact-sheets/underage-drinking

12 U.S.Department of Health and Human Services (HHS),
Substance Abuse and Mental Health Services Administration
(SAMHSA). (2017). Report to Congress on the Prevention
and Reduction of Underage Drinking

13 Ibid.

14 Ibid.

15 Underage Drinking. National Institute on Alcohol Abuse and Alcoholism. Retrieved from https://www.niaaa.nih.gov/publications/brochures-and-fact-sheets/underage-drinking

16 How to tell if your child is drinking alcohol. (SAMHSA). Retrieved at https://www.samhsa.gov/underage-drinking/parent-resources/how-tell-if-your-child-drinking-alcohol

17 Johnson, L.D., Miech, R.A.,O'Malley, P.M., Bachman, J.G., & Patrick, M.E. (2020). Monitoring the Future National Survey Results on Drug use 1975-2019. Overview, Key Findings on Adolescent Drug Use. Ann Arbor. Institute for Social Research, University of Michigan

18 Ibid.

19 NIDA. (2018, June 6). Electronic Cigarettes (E-cigarettes). Retrieved from https://www.drugabuse.gov/publications/drugfacts/electronic-cigarettes-e-cigarettes

20 Ibid.

21 U. S. Department of Health & Human Services. Adolescents and Tobacco: Tips for Parents. Retrieved from https://www.hhs.gov/ash/aah/adolescent-development/substance-use/drugs/tobacco/tips-for-parents/index.html

22 Drug Enforcement Administration (2017). Drugs of Abuse: A DEA Resource Guide. Retrieved from https://www.dea.gov/sites/default/files/drug_of_abuse.pdf

23 NIDA. (2018, June 7). Heroin. Retrieved from https://www.drugabuse.gov/publications/drugfacts/heroin

24 NIDA. (2018, June7) Heroin. Retrieved from https://www.drugabuse.gov/publications/drugfacts/heroin

25 Ibid.

26 Ibid.

27 Johnson, L.D., Miech, R.A., O'Malley, P.M., Bachman, J.G.,& Patrick, M.E. (2020). Monitoring the Future National Survey Results on Drug Use, 1975-2019. Overview, key findings on adolescent drug use. Ann Arbor. Institute for Social Research, University of Michigan.

28 NIDA. (2018, June 7) Prescription Opioids. Retrieved from https://www.drugabuse.gov/publications/drugfacts/prescription-opioids

29 Ibid.

30 Ibid.

31 NIDA. (2016, May 6) Cocaine. Retrieved from https://www.drugabuse.gov/publications/research-reports/cocaine on 2019, May 26

32 Ibid.

33 Johnson, L.D., Miech, R.A., O'Malley, P.M., Bachman, J.G., & Patrick, M.E. Monitoring the Future National Survey Results on Drug Use, 1975-2019. Overview, Key Findings on Adolescent Drug Use. Ann Arbor. Institute for Social Research, University of Michigan.

34 NIDA. (2013, September 19). Methamphetamine. Retrieved from https://www.drugabuse.gov/publications/research-reports/methamphetamine

35 NIDA. (2018, February 5). Synthetic cathinones ("bath salts"). Retrieved from https://www.drugabuse.gov/publica-

tions/drugfacts/synthetic-cathinones-bath-salts

36 DEA. Drugs of Abuse, A DEA Resource Guide. Retrieved from https://www.dea.gov/sites/default/2018-06/drugs_of_abuse.pdf

37 NIDA. (2018, June 6) Prescription stimulants. Retrieved from https://www.drugabuse.gov/publications/drugfacts/prescription-stimulants

38 NIDA. (2018, March 6). Prescription CNS depressants. Retrieved from https://www.drugabuse.gov/publications/drugfacts/prescription-cns-depressants.

39 NIDA. (2015, February 1). Hallucinogens and dissociative drugs. Retrieved from https://www.drugabuse.gov/publications/research-reports/hallucinogens-dissociative-drugs

40 NIDA. (2012, July 1). Inhalants. Retrieved from https://www.drugabuse.com/publications/research-reports/inhalants

41 NIDA. (2018, June 6). MDMA (ecstasy.molly). Retrieved from https://www.drugabuse.gov/publications/drugfacts/mdma-ecstasy-molly

42 Warning Signs of Teen Self-Injury. Newport Academy. Retrieved from https://www.newportacademcy.com/resources/mental-health/self-injury

43 American Academy of Child and Adolescent Psychiatry. Eating Disorder in Teens. Retrieved from https://www.aacaporg/AACAP/Families_And_Youth/Facts_For_Families/FFF-Guide/Teenagers-With-Eating-Disorders-002.aspx

44 Ibid.

45 Ibid.

46 Ibid.

47 Teen Eating Disorders. Newport Academy. Retrieved from https://www.newportacademy.com/treatment/teen-eating-disorders/

48 Gaming Disorder. Newport Academy. Retired from https://www.newportacademy.com/resources/mental-health/gaming-disorder/

49 Newport Academy. The Latest on Teen Cell Phone Addiction. Retrieved from https://www.newportacademy.com/resources/mental-health/teen-cell-phone-addiction/

50 National Highway Traffic Safety Administration. Distracted Driving. Retrieved from https:www.nhtsa.gov/road-safety/teen-driving

51 Ibid.

52 Newport Academy. The Latest on Teen Cell Phone Addiction. Retrieved from https://www.newportacademy.com/resources/mental-health/teen-cell-phone-addiction/

53 NIDA. (2014, January 14). Principles of Adolescent Substance Use Disorder Treatment: A Research-Based Guide. Retrieved from https://www.drugabuse.gov/publications/principles-adolescent-substance-use-disorder-treatment-research-based-guide

54 NIDA. 2020, June 3. Is legally mandated treatment effective? Retrieved for https://www.drugabuse.gov/publications/principles-drug-abuse-treatment-criminal-justice-populations-research-based/legally-mandated-treatment-effective

55 Center for Substance Abuse Treatment. What Is Substance Abuse Treatment? A booklet for Families. HHS Publication No. (SMA) 14-4126. Rockvill, MD: Substance Abuse and Mental Health Services Administration, 2004

56 National Institute on Drug Abuse. Seeking Drug Abuse Treatment: Know what to ask. Publication No. 13-7764. Revised June 2013

57 Ibid.

58 NIDA (2014, January 14). Principles of Adolescent Substance Abuse Disorder Treatment. A Research-Based Guide. Retrieved from https://www.drugabuse.gov/publications/principles-adolescent-substance-use-disorder-treatment-research-based-guide